400 Tips

on

Autism

and

Leadership

Understand, Lead and Grow People with Autism at Work, Home, and Life

Trevor Pacelli

Patty Pacelli

Lonnie Pacelli

400 Tips on Autism and Leadership – growingupautistic.com

Editing by Patty Pacelli

Published by Pacelli Publishing
9905 Lake Washington Blvd. NE, #D-103
Bellevue, Washington 98004
PacelliPublishing.com

ISBN-10: 1- 1-933750-53-7
ISBN-13: 978-1-933750-53-8

Table of Contents

15 Tips to Help Employees with Autism Be Rock Stars

Lonnie Pacelli

LonniePacelli.com

The Israeli Defense Force (IDF) Special intelligence Unit 9900 is dedicated to everything related to geography, including mapping, interpretation of aerial and satellite photographs and space research. Within this unit there is a small unit of highly qualified soldiers, who have remarkable visual and analytic capabilities. They can detect even the smallest details, undetectable to most people. These soldiers all have one thing in common; they are on the autism spectrum. Their job is to take visual materials from satellite images and sensors in the air. With the help of officers and decoding tools, they analyze the images and find specific things necessary to provide the best data to those planning missions. The IDF has found that soldiers with autism can focus for longer periods of time than their neurotypical (non-autistic) counterparts (source: IDF Blog).

SAP, a worldwide leader in enterprise software solutions, is tapping into the extraordinary observation and concentration characteristics of people with autism to do software testing. SAP has pledged that 1% of their global workforce will be autistic by 2020 (source: SAP).

Organizations such as IDF, SAP, Microsoft, Walgreens, and Freddie Mac have recognized the extraordinary strengths that many people on the Autism Spectrum possess. This is not a corporate goodwill gesture; these organizations are looking to improve bottom line results and see people with autism as a means to help them get there. The Center for Disease Control (CDC) reports that about 1 in 68 children have been identified with autism spectrum disorder (ASD), that it occurs 1 in 42 among boys and 1 in 189 among girls and occurs among all racial, socioeconomic, and ethnic groups (source: CDC). This is up from 1 in 150 occurrences in the year 2000.

Our son Trevor was diagnosed with high-functioning autism at age 5. It initially showed as delayed speech and continued with social awkwardness and other emotional and communication difficulties. Even as a toddler, Trevor showed tremendous abilities to focus through activities like puzzles and, in his passion areas, he could memorize and recite the most detailed of facts. As he grew, his passions shifted to movies and photography. During his first two years in junior college he majored in film studies and eventually got a BA cum laude in film & media studies from Arizona State University. Trevor now works for my wife Patty and me where he focuses on movie reviews, photography, and marketing his and other books on autism.

Having Trevor as an employee has been a terrific experience for all of us, but at the same time I've learned that after 30+ years working for companies such as Microsoft and Accenture that a leader needs to be mindful of how a person with autism thinks and works. The changes I needed to make weren't massive enough to completely retool my leadership toolbox; but they were important enough that I had to consciously act to ensure our styles meshed.

If your company is embarking on an initiative to hire more people with autism, now is the time to act. Take a look at these 15 tips which have worked for me and may help you create the most supportive and productive environment for your employee with autism (Note: there are two schools of thought as to how to refer to a person with autism. There is the "person first" camp who say "person with autism." There is the "identify first" camp who say "autistic person." Neither term is universally correct nor incorrect. I use both terms with no intent to offend).

1. Expect different processing paces
Some people with autism process information at a different pace and may not "think on their feet" well. Allow the employee some time to process requests and feedback before discussing in depth. Sending an email first with a verbal follow-up is something that works well with Trevor.

2. Watch the non-verbals
Non-verbal social communication, i.e., facial expression and eye contact, can be lacking in people with autism. Don't over-interpret this as rudeness, unhappiness, or some other negative feeling. Also recognize that the employee may not pick up on non-verbal cues from you or co-workers.

3. Minimize unplanned interruptions (even fun ones)
"Hey, birthday party in the break room right now" is fun for many neurotypicals but for the person with autism it can be an unwelcome disruption of his schedule that he has already worked out. Be conscious of unplanned interruptions by giving advance notice where possible and allowing for the employee to opt out if not business critical. At the same time, don't exclude the employee from activities--this could lead to hurt feelings.

4. Accept employee input on workstation setup
Because many people with autism have heightened sensitivity to things like sight, touch, smell and sound, their workspace environment could have a significant impact on their ability to be productive. Allow the employee to have a voice in their workstation setup, i.e., wearing headphones, reduced lighting, or working farther away from common areas, which will help him be more productive.

5. Develop quantifiable objectives with monthly "dones" check-ins
This works particularly well with Trevor. We do a monthly meeting where we review his

overall objectives and what will get done during the month to get him closer to each objective. At month-end we review what actually got done that month, provide feedback, and set the dones for the next month. See more about the dones process here.

6. Make use of mentors to help with each objective
Trevor has specific mentors for his photography, movie reviews, and book marketing lines of business who advise him on his work, provide feedback, and answer questions. These mentor sessions have proven to be effective, helping him tap into subject matter expertise that we can't provide, and he has learned how to discern and incorporate input into his work.

7. Provide more written and visual instruction, less verbal instruction
Generally speaking, people with autism are visual learners and more easily comprehend ideas and direction when they are able to see them and ask questions versus just hearing them. Another helpful technique is to ask the employee to write out a verbal instruction then discuss what was written to ensure clear understanding.

8. Use calm tone of voice
Loud or stern voices tend to rattle people with autism more than neurotypical people. Being mindful of using a calm voice will help minimize confusion and angst.

9. Use "feedback sliders"
Accepting and incorporating both positive and constructive feedback is absolutely crucial to career growth and the employee shouldn't be exempt from feedback. An effective feedback technique is what I call the "feedback slider"; one positive piece of feedback, (the bottom of the bun), then one constructive piece of feedback (the meat), followed up with a re-iteration of the positive piece of feedback (the top of the bun). This bite-sized approach is easier for the person with autism to absorb and reduces over-reaction to constructive feedback.

10. Encourage being the "go-to" person on some topic
Trevor is my "go-to" person when I need input on how a person with autism will react to my articles, presentations, and videos. He knows that I rely on his input and that my work product will be better because of his perspective. Identify an area where the employee excels, promote him or her as a subject matter expert with your team, and encourage the rest of your team to utilize the expertise. Just try not to interrupt them when asking.

11. Be blunt on what, when, and why
Autistic people tend to be very literal and are at their best when they are not left to decode unspoken or "between the lines" communication. When defining assignments, ensure there is clarity on what needs to be produced, what the deliverable should look like, why it is important, and when it needs to be done by. Asking the employee to create a mock-up of the deliverable and reviewing the mock-up is a great way to ensure alignment and minimizes rework due to confusion.

12. Keep appointments and meetings on schedule and give advance notice on schedule changes

People with autism typically are very schedule-minded and have difficulty with unexpected schedule changes. At the same time, there's no such thing as perfect schedule adherence. Try to give advance notice where possible of meetings or projects that will run over or if you might be late for a meeting with him. Also take time to explain why a schedule change is needed; this can help the employee get on board with the change. If you're a leader who typically runs late or doesn't respect meeting end times, this might be a good opportunity to work on your time management skills :-).

13. Allow the employee to opt out of social events

Socializing can be work for many people with autism. Trevor typically runs out of steam after about two hours of socializing, particularly if he's actively engaging in the socialization. Encourage the employee to join in on social events, but allow him to opt out or to leave if he is feeling overwhelmed or stressed.

14. Don't underestimate intelligence or ability to deliver

People with autism are differently abled; they're not less intelligent or less able to get something done. They simply march to their own beat. Every time I underestimated Trevor's ability to do something he proved me wrong. Don't be shy about challenging the employee with a big task or aggressive deadline. Chances are he will rise up to the challenge.

15. Embrace the differences

Co-worker and manager attitudes and opinions towards people with behavioral and social differences is foundational to a healthy workforce. Creating a welcome work environment benefits not only the employee with autism but the team as a whole. Understanding the differences and assigning tasks that capitalize on them not only creates a happier team but drives greater results.

1 in 68 are born on the autism spectrum. These children grow into adults and will be a key workforce asset. If you are or will be managing someone with autism, get prepared so you can get the most out of the relationship and help your employee with autism thrive and drive results for you and your organization.

Six-Word Lessons for Autism Friendly Workplaces

100 Lessons for Employers and Employees to Succeed Together

Patty Pacelli

GrowingUpAutistic.com

Introduction

Our second child Trevor was born in December of 1992, and diagnosed with PDD-NOS (Pervasive Development Disorder-Not Otherwise Specified) while in kindergarten. We learned about autism throughout his childhood, and relied on our public school district's teachers, counselors and specialists, whom I see as true heroes. There were challenges along the way, and we learned as much as we could. Trevor graduated from high school right on schedule with a B average. It was a proud, exciting time, but in some ways even more of an "unknown" than when he was diagnosed with autism in kindergarten.

I am writing this book to help build awareness that as children with autism become adults, they need to live independently and support themselves with meaningful work, a dream that all parents have for their kids. This book is for individuals with autism either looking for jobs or currently working, and for employers, human resource managers, small business owners, supervisors and co-workers of adults with autism.

This book contains 100 short lessons to give both employees and employers guidelines on helping adults with autism find careers that fulfill and support them, and thrive in the workplace while benefiting their employers with their skills and talents. I hope this helps many adults with autism and employers to find well-fitting, meaningful and productive working relationships.

Acknowledgements

Thank-you to the experts in the field of autism and employment who so willingly met with me and shared their knowledge and opinions: Kim Kimbell, Sara Gardner, Lisa Iland Hilbert, Manfred Seidler, Michael Goodwill, Garry Burge, Ben Wilshire and Elaine Duncan.

I am grateful to the board members of the Seattle Children's Autism Guild for their continual interest and support. They have inspired and encouraged me to help young adults with autism find fulfilling careers: Andrea Duffield, Karen Kaizuka, Susan Steckler, Elijah Winfrey, Lisa Iland Hilbert and Julie O'Brien. Thanks also to Seattle Children's Autism Center representatives, Katrina Davis, Megen Strand and Tammy Mitchel for direction, ideas and support.

I also appreciate the help and information from Paige Morrow of Extraordinary Ventures and Jeri Kendle of the Southwest Autism Research & Resource Center. Both of these organizations are doing exciting things to help adults with autism find meaningful work.

I dedicate this book to my husband Lonnie, who first had the idea of the "autism friendly workplace," my daughter Briana, who was and still is the best big sister anyone with autism could have, and for Trevor, who has amazed us with his accomplishments and growth, and continues the fight to live and succeed in a different, difficult world.

Terminology

While working on this book, I heard about an opinion in the autism and disability community that disabilities should be referred to in "person first" language, i.e., "person with autism" rather than "autistic person."

I did a survey on the subject on our Growing Up Autistic Facebook page and received comments that were split about fifty/fifty on which way they preferred, and some said it didn't matter.

Because of my survey results, and my own opinion as a parent and writer, I have chosen to use both terms in this book, partially because of grammar and word count considerations. I hope the choice of wording will not affect the message and intent of the book, and that these differences of opinion will not divide a community that should be working together to support all individuals with disabilities.

The Need for Autism Friendly Workplaces

1. Traits of autism hinder job possibilities.

My son Trevor applied for dozens of summer jobs during his high school and college years. He was occasionally called for interviews, but usually didn't get the jobs; I believe largely because of his autism. Eventually, he found two summer jobs, and his work was stellar. I hope to help other young adults find meaningful employment.

2. Children with autism quickly become adults.

Research is clear that the number of children being diagnosed with autism spectrum disorders is rising. The maturing of these children will lead to more and more adults entering the workforce in the coming years. This book is a springboard for discussing how companies and the autism community can work together to hire these individuals, resulting in productivity and success for all.

3. Employment statistics can be quite discouraging.

For autistic adults aged 21-25, approximately one-half (53.4%) with an autism spectrum disorder have ever worked for pay outside the home since leaving high school, according to a 2013 study from the *Journal of the American Academy of Child & Adolescent Psychiatry* (jaacap.com) by Dr. Paul Shattuck and his team.

4. Autism employment is lowest among disabilities.

In a national study of young adults who had received any type of special services in high school, the adults with autism spectrum disorders (ASDs) had the lowest employment rate of all other disabilities. The study concluded that there is a particular difficulty with finding work for the autistic population. (jaacap.com)

5. Pay for autistic workers is low.

Adults with autism typically earn less than others in the workforce. In addition, studies show that autistic employees are limited to fewer occupational types. Dr. Shattuck's study also found that conversational abilities and higher household income result in higher-paying jobs. (jaacap.com)

6. Work is a basic human need.

Human beings were made to work, and adults with autism are no different. Employment leads to a better mood, higher self-esteem, and improved physical health; and allows autistic adults to further develop in their skills and understanding. Our son Trevor liked being around people and the enjoyed the feeling of accomplishment at his jobs.

7. More barriers exist for autistic employees.

Individuals with autism experience additional hindrances in finding and retaining employment. A 2013 article by Tamar Najarian lists these barriers as: sensory overload issues; problems showing emotions; inadequate language; social awkwardness;

inability to handle large crowds; need for things to be a certain way; and lack of proper mental transition into adulthood. (emaxhealth.com)

Career Preparation for Parents and Children

8. Start early and involve the family.

Parents should begin thinking about employment for children with autism when they are young. Involving them in household chores, volunteer work, and other projects will prepare them for employment, says Michael Goodwill, manager of transition services at PROVAIL in Seattle. From a young age, Trevor did weekly chores and took care of his own needs as much as possible.

9. Plan for employment in elementary school.

Career planning can start as soon as children begin developing interests, at age 14 or sooner, say transition specialists. Taking note of interests, especially their passions, can help them pursue and cultivate them. If they talk about dreams that seem unrealistic, encourage them anyway. Trevor told us at age 9 that he wanted to be a movie director; he eventually got a film degree.

10. Teach early independence for later rewards.

When raising Trevor, we always hoped that he would be able to live on his own when he grew up. Because he is high functioning, and because we worked toward that goal from his childhood, he is now living in a university residence hall, and continues to live independently.

11. Independent living can increase employment rate.

The goal of independent living is important, and studies have shown that it leads to great employment success. "Autistic individuals are six times more likely to find and retain a job if they live alone or with a partner, run a household, and have previously held any job for longer than six months," according to emaxhealth.com.

12. Find out about skills and preferences.

Autistic children should job-shadow as early as middle school, and look for job sampling opportunities, volunteering and internships, to learn about various work environments. They should also cultivate life skills such as traveling and using public transportation. (*Life Journey Through Autism: a Guide to Transition to Adulthood*, OAR and SARRC)

13. Try to see challenges as strengths.

While watching for strengths, be aware of subject areas or tasks that are challenging or difficult for your child. Keep them in mind when envisioning the future, but consider how a challenge at home could be a strength in the workplace. Trevor was hypersensitive about being on time, which caused conflicts with the family occasionally, but it became a strength when he had his first job.

How to Find the Best Jobs

14. School-to-work programs foster success.

School-to-work programs are government-funded programs that give students with disabilities opportunities to work with contracted employment agencies who match company job openings to student workers. Students can participate in these programs while in high school, or directly after high school, as part of a school district transition program.

15. Transition programs lead to successful employment.

Transition programs that guide students from high school to the workplace are "tremendously successful" in King County, Washington, according to Goodwill. His agency, PROVAIL, saw 60 to 70 percent of students in their school-to-work program find jobs in the past year.

16. Transition specialists and businesses work together.

Businesses are usually very receptive to hiring employees with disabilities, according to Goodwill. He said they often create specific jobs to fit employees and hire them for the times and hours they are available. As long as companies have the right information, they are usually happy to hire individuals with disabilities.

17. Know that being older has advantages.

Autistic adults "who are older, come from households of higher income, and are higher functioning in society" are more likely to find jobs, according to emaxhealth.com. It's harder for young adults with autism to transition to adulthood in general, so this also makes it difficult to retain employment.

18. Alternative methods may lead to employment.

Along with early preparation at home, and transition and school-to-work programs, Elaine Duncan, a psychotherapist who works with adults with autism, suggests that a great way for those on the spectrum to find jobs is to use "back door methods," such as advocates and any acquaintances who can help them network and lead them to the right jobs.

19. Employees should agree with company values.

Because people with autism are more "black and white" in their thinking, and usually have strong opinions and beliefs, it's very important that their values align with their company's values, according to Duncan. If they have a strong positive opinion about a company's core philosophy, they will be happier and more productive working for that company.

20. Ideal employment opportunities usually involve independence.

People with autism are usually not highly team-oriented, and prefer to be on their own, and Duncan finds that the vast majority of her clients on the spectrum find work in the computer industry. She has also found that individuals with autism are successful as tutors, because they enjoy using their intelligence and expertise while working one-on-one with students.

21. Many fields are compatible for autism.

Emaxhealth.com recommends jobs in the information technology field, among others. They suggest computer programmer, engineer, drafter, commercial artist, photographer, graphic designer, web designer, cartoonist, librarian, mechanic, craftsman, technical repairman, carpenter, welder, building maintenance, accountant, statistician, and journalist as good jobs for those with autism.

22. There are jobs for nonverbal employees.

Jobs for nonverbal or nonspeaking autistic adults include janitor, store stocker, library helper, factory assembly worker, copy shop helper, warehouse helper, landscaping, data entry, and office helper. Any job that doesn't require communicating verbally with others is a possibility. (emaxhealth.com)

23. It's OK to avoid some jobs.

While everyone is different, there are some jobs that are simply not suitable for most people with autism. Emaxhealth.com lists these jobs to avoid: cashier, waiter/waitress, casino dealer, taxi dispatcher, ticket agent, market trader, auctioneer, receptionist, and most customer service jobs.

24. Family businesses offer alternative work opportunities.

For a different approach from traditional job-hunting, creative parents can help their children with autism find appropriate jobs by starting businesses that will use their child's strengths, and possibly train them to eventually take over the business and run it on their own or with help from other employees.

25. Starting a new business channels enthusiasm.

Autistic individuals should consider starting a business, because autistic people "have so much drive, enthusiasm and intelligence," Duncan says, so it's nice to channel that into a business venture. It "gets them out of that box they don't fit into." She said, "Doing something original allows them to thrive with their differences."

26. Joining with others can create opportunities.

A group of parents in Chapel Hill, North Carolina created several small businesses to provide employment for their children with autism. Their nonprofit, Extraordinary Ventures employs over 40 adults with autism and other disabilities in their own event center. Workers do laundry, make candles, and many other tasks. (extraordinaryventures.org)

27. Training programs exist for autistic adults.

Southwest Autism Research & Resource Center has a program called CulinaryWorks (culinaryworks.com) that teaches cooking and food service skills to adults with autism, then helps them launch careers by arranging internships or hiring them for their own coffee shops and catering companies. SARRC has placed over 75 students in job positions.

28. Good training can lead to entrepreneurship.

A student in Arizona's CulinaryWorks program completed specialized training, interned at a bakery, took private lessons with a pastry chef, and has now launched his own business. Because of help from a local autism center and other volunteers and businesses willing to get involved, this adult on the autism spectrum is self-employed and supporting himself.

29. Many companies have disability hiring programs.

It is not uncommon for large companies to specifically focus on hiring certain numbers of employees with disabilities, according to Goodwill. Companies value these employees' talents and want to be more diverse by employing all types of people. Many of these jobs are high-paying, professional jobs with good career potential.

ADA Laws and Rules for Work

30. All parties must understand discrimination laws.

The Americans with Disabilities Act (ADA), enacted in 1990, states in the Title I employment section that qualified applicants with disabilities may not be discriminated against in application procedures, hiring, advancement and discharge, workers compensation, job training and other terms and privileges of employment. (U.S. Department of Labor)

31. Discrimination can surface in various forms.

Title I of the ADA says that discrimination may include limiting or classifying an applicant or employee in an adverse way, denying employment to someone who is qualified, not making reasonable accommodations, or not advancing employees with disabilities. Knowing these rights ensures that everyone is treated fairly. (U.S. Department of Labor)

32. Understand the Section 503 Rehabilitation Act.

Section 503, from 1973, adds more specific rules about employers with federal contracts or subcontracts. If contracts are more than $10,000, employers must take affirmative action to hire, retain and promote qualified individuals with disabilities. Those seeking employment should be aware of this provision. (U.S. Department of Labor)

33. 503 changes will provide more benefits.

Section 503 is undergoing clarifying updates which should benefit employees with disabilities. The new law will explicitly require nondiscrimination and affirmative action. Also, the definition of a "qualified individual with a disability" will be broadened to someone "unable to perform a major life activity that the average person can perform," which would include job duties. (U.S. Department of Labor)

34. Interviewees need not address medical issues.

Applicants with autism should keep in mind that the changes in the 503 law will prohibit any medical inquiries before making an offer. Employers may only ask about abilities to perform job-related functions. Medical exams or inquiries will only be permitted if "job related and consistent with business necessity." (U.S. Department of Labor)

Best Interview Practices for the Employer

35. Treat autistic people like anyone else.

Employers are not allowed to ask an interviewee about a disability, or even treat him like he has a disability, says human resources consultant Kim Kimbell. Employers may only ask the interviewee if he is able to perform the functions of the job. Disclosing the disability is up to the prospective employee, but he certainly does not have to do so during the interview.

36. Always look for the best fit.

Consider where people with autism will fit best, says Duncan, a former recruiter who now counsels adults on the spectrum. They should be placed in jobs with the appropriate co-workers, environments and job duties. People will be happiest and most productive in jobs for which they are well-suited.

37. Let the applicant demonstrate his skills.

An autistic person can often most effectively show his skills through a sample activity. Offering a practice activity, such as proofing a sample document for an editing position. This can help employers make more accurate hiring decisions. It can be difficult for autistic people to "sell themselves" and put their skills and attributes into words, even if they are excellent candidates.

Interview Tips for People with Autism

38. Consider working with an interview coach.

Interview coaches can coordinate with employers to get questions in advance, coach interviewees in the actual interview space. This has made a significant difference in helping applicants feel prepared for interviews, says Lisa Iland Hilbert of Social Bridge, which provides interview coaching. Coaches give interviewees lists of topics to avoid and points to highlight when interviewing.

39. Memorize and use an elevator pitch.

People with autism often have good memorizing skills, according to Hilbert, who works with autistic adults. It's easy for them to prepare a 30-second "elevator pitch," to tell prospective employers about their talents, skills, experience and abilities, and why they are best for the job. They should prepare answers for questions such as, "Tell us about yourself," and "Why do you want this job?"

40. Prepare something unique for the interview.

If autistic applicants can give a prospective employer a method for demonstrating his skills that is more creative than describing them verbally, it will help the employer to better identify his abilities. Hilbert suggests applicants prepare video clips, websites or portfolios of work relevant to the position to more easily show their skills.

41. Don't talk about autism during interview.

As discussed earlier, applicants with autism do not have to disclose any disabilities at the interview. They should learn the questions that interviewers are not allowed to ask, and only talk about their job qualifications. Sara Gardner, program manager of the Autism Spectrum Navigators at Bellevue College says, "Wait until you get the job to disclose."

42. Exceptions to nondisclosure at the interview.

One reason to disclose autism during an interview would be when someone simply "doesn't present well," said Duncan, because of differences in communication and social skills. Disclosing autism might help the interviewer understand the reason for lower than average social skills, allowing the interviewer to focus on the skills necessary to do the job.

Reasonable Accommodations for Employers to Offer

43. Accommodations help employer and employee succeed.

In the ideal scenario, giving autistic employees accommodations would help the company run more effectively while helping autistic employees to be productive, leading to better products or services and more profit. All parties should work together to allow autistic employees to be productive without sacrificing the work environment for others.

44. Options for accommodations make a difference.

All onboarding employees should be given a survey or menu of options, suggests Hilbert, asking their preferences for things like sound, light, physical work space, type of communication desired, methods for performance appraisals and more. This allows autistic employees to simply state their preferences along with everyone else, without feeling different or singled out.

45. Workplace design can work for everyone.

The concept of "Universal Design" makes workplaces comfortable and accommodating for those with autism as well as those with other disabilities, while not infringing on employees without disabilities, Gardner said. This format makes it easy for people with autism to fit in to the work environment and do their jobs in the most productive way possible.

46. Step-by-step instructions ensure clarity.

People with autism need clear, step-by-step instructions so they know exactly what is expected of them, along with very detailed job descriptions they can refer to often. They are not less intelligent; they just process differently and are often visual learners, so the more clearly directions are spelled out, the better they will be at following those directions.

47. More showing than telling is effective.

Trevor's supervisor at his maintenance job, Manfred Seidler, observed that Trevor learned better by being shown how to do something, rather than just told verbally. When he showed Trevor how to lock up all the doors in the building, he physically walked through the locations with him, and after one time, "he got it," and never forgot the process.

48. Visual tools make a big difference.

Anything that is more visual and demonstrative will help autistic employees better understand what is expected of them on the job. Trevor said that calendars with deadlines were especially beneficial to him. Videos and slide shows are also helpful ways to teach an autistic person, rather than simply giving verbal instructions.

49. Accommodate sensory issues to reduce overload.

Many autistic people have physical sensitivities that can make workplaces difficult. Sara Gardner, who works in an office and has sensory processing differences, has difficulty with bright lights, as well as office sounds such as typing, so she has arranged for the overhead lights in her office to be turned off, and often wears earplugs on the job.

50. Autistic workers need more private space.

It can be helpful for those with autism to work behind a closed door, even for part of the day. Sara Gardner has an accommodation for her office mate to work elsewhere for part of each day; a conference room could also meet this need. Because this can come across as rude or standoffish, managers should educate all employees to show tolerance and understanding.

51. Quiet surroundings lead to better focus.

While everyone is different, most people with autism spectrum disorders have some type of sensitivity to sound, even soft, continuous sounds, such as typing. Duncan says even road noise, fans and conversations can "drive them crazy because they can't filter out sounds like other people." They can get headaches and lose focus from these sounds. Ear protection can help.

52. All employees should respect others' differences.

Although an autistic employee may be allowed to wear headphones while he works, Gardner notes that this can send a social cue that she doesn't want to talk or socialize, so she could be considered rude, unsociable, or not team-oriented. Managers can encourage tolerance and open communication among all.

53. Loud music can be especially distressing.

People with autism can be very sensitive to loud music playing in the background, whether in a retail store, restaurant, warehouse or office. Public or work spaces would be more autism-friendly if they played the music low enough for people to talk, which would be appreciated by not only employees, but any customers with autism as well.

54. Working location can make or break.

Even if they aren't bothered by noise, autistic employees often work best when they have a dedicated space that isn't too close to other people. Hilbert suggested sitting on the outer edge of a group of office cubicles, or in a separate area, toward the edge of a larger area or manufacturing floor. Working farther away from coffee and lunch break areas is usually helpful, too, to keep from distractions.

55. Regular risk assessments keep everyone safe.

Garry Burge, an adult with Asperger's and an advocate for working adults on the spectrum, says that when autistic employees are working with machinery and equipment, there should be regular risk assessments and check-ins to make sure they are using the equipment properly and being safe.

56. Employees need guidance in question protocol.

Some adults on the spectrum need guidance to ask questions or get clarification, according to Hilbert. Some are hesitant to ask, while others ask too frequently. Creating a flowchart illustrating the types of questions appropriate for HR, supervisor, job coach, or colleague, can help employees to direct questions appropriately.

57. Provide a predictable framework for feedback.

While autistic employees need to get used to the culture of feedback, Hilbert said they also can benefit from the structure of knowing that it will be given at an expected time, place and method. Something like a weekly check-in, with both positive feedback as well as suggestions, given at the same time and place, is a good way to approach performance appraisals.

58. Advanced notice of recognition is helpful.

While most employees love to have a surprise award or kudos given, those on the spectrum would prefer to know ahead of time that they will be recognized. They will appreciate advanced notice of any type of event to recognize or thank them or others, especially if it will interrupt their usual workday routine.

59. One-on-one settings maximize learning.

When learning something new, Hilbert says that many times autistic employees "need more one-on-one attention," rather than being taught as part of a group. This is because of the differences in processing, and the sensitivity to distractions around them. An offer to show them something individually will lead to better productivity.

60. Direct communication methods are most effective.

Most people with autism communicate best in writing, according to Gardner. She suggests that supervisors write out very clear and direct instructions, whether in a job description, an assignment, or a performance appraisal. Spell out the specific desired behavior, such as, "Be ready to start working at exactly 9:00," rather than "Don't be late."

61. Allowing extra adjustment time is crucial.

Whether it is a change in location, routine, responsibilities or reporting, a person with autism usually needs at least twice as much time as his peers to get used to the difference, because of the extra emotions to process, according to Duncan. He will still perform his job as usual, but he may take longer to adjust and need to discuss the changes more than other employees.

Accommodations that can Help Autistic Employees

62. After hiring is best disclosure time.

The only way to receive job accommodations is to disclose the disability to the appropriate people, usually the HR manager and supervisor. For an employee with autism, meeting everyday demands without accommodations can be difficult to impossible, so disclosure of autism once hired is highly recommended.

63. Coaching can yield support and strategies.

PROVAIL is an example of a coaching company that uses a team approach, involving companies, the applicant's family and others to learn as much as possible about the employee and the working environment. Job coaches should be thoughtful and observe and get to know the potential employee's strengths and work pace to help match him with the right job, said Goodwill.

64. Coaching can also help at work.

A job coach can stay involved indefinitely once someone is hired, and can be there as much as needed to advocate, create task lists and schedules, and communicate with both employee and employer to address any issues, said Goodwill. Because job coaches also help place employees, they often will already have a relationship with the employer.

65. Behind-the-scenes coaching is valuable.

For employees with autism, coaches can help even if they are not working with the employee on the job site. They can meet regularly on- or off-site to check in, even when things are going fine, according to Duncan. Regular coach-employee meetings ward off potential problems or misunderstandings, and the coach can ask questions regularly to make sure all is going well.

Benefits of Hiring People with Autism

66. Autistic employees' passions lead to productivity.

Because autistic individuals usually have intense, specific interests, the best jobs are those that allow them to be involved with those interests. For example, Gardner once had a job in sales. Selling isn't normally a strength in an autistic person, but because she was passionate about the product, she enjoyed the job and was very successful at it.

67. Strong interests make them work hard.

Hiring an autistic employee who is perfectly suited to the job because of an intense, passionate interest results in a win-win situation because when someone works on something he enjoys and has extensive knowledge in, he will "leap tall buildings," Gardner says, and be "one of the most productive people you would ever want to meet."

68. They love to be on time.

Like many people with autism, our son Trevor was always very aware of time, and wanted to stick to a schedule. He owned and used a watch from preschool on, and that attention to timeliness helped him when he had a job. Because autistic individuals thrive on routine, schedules, and predictability, they will rarely, if ever, be late to work or meetings, which is a dream for employers.

69. They work when nobody is watching.

When Trevor worked in maintenance for a church, we often received comments from his coworkers who had seen him doing heavy landscape work outside in the heat. Trevor didn't know anyone saw him, but he nevertheless worked hard when alone, never slacking or resting. It was that focus and commitment to do whatever he was asked that made him a model employee.

70. They find comfort in daily routines.

Trevor's supervisor referred to the routine of locking up every door in the building as Trevor's "security blanket." Autistic employees will perform well with tasks that involve routine and repetition, which are easy and comforting to them. Trevor also said the comfort of a routine helped him endure the other demands of the job.

71. They can be the most reliable.

Trevor's supervisor told him he was his "right-hand man." He said Trevor was more reliable than many of his other employees, and he could always count on him to do his work, that he took literally no supervision, and that he didn't have to check up on him. "As a supervisor, that's huge," Seidler said.

72. Autistic people have strong intrinsic motivation.

Trevor says that whenever he was told to do something at work, he just did it. When working in the kitchen at a summer camp, his fear of possible negative consequences, a typical trait for autistic individuals, actually motivated him to do his best. His supervisor was impressed with his commitment and that he finished his tasks so quickly.

73. Intense focus comes naturally to them.

Autistic people's intensity can be an asset that helps them focus on the task at hand. Trevor's extreme focusing ability allowed him to wash huge piles of dishes quickly without stopping or complaining. His kitchen supervisor remarked that Trevor was "like a machine" and couldn't believe how hard and fast he worked. Trevor said the repetition was comforting to him and he "just plowed right through it."

Be Aware of Unique Autistic Traits

74. Training should be given about autism.

The more training and education that takes place for managers and supervisors regarding how autistic individuals are wired, the better the work environment will be for everyone, according to Hilbert. Managers can have a big impact on acceptance among all employees by teaching awareness of the characteristics of autism, which will lead to better teamwork and productivity.

75. Autistic individuals can bring enormous creativity.

Workers with autism can have imaginations that are well above average. Managers should take advantage of this when looking for creative ideas or new ways to solve problems. If they give autistic team members opportunities to share their ideas, those ideas can lead to brilliant new concepts.

76. Autistic individuals need more processing time.

Because of so many things happening in their heads, those with autism find it difficult to verbalize with the same speed and clarity as others. They need coworkers and managers to give them a little extra time to explain and share their thoughts, and it will be worth the wait.

77. Emotions can be extreme at times.

A common fear of employers is that autistic employees don't have good emotional regulation. However, Gardner has found that a high percentage of those on the spectrum are calmer than the average employee. The difference is that when upset, an autistic person will show it more. However, they are also more energetic, enthusiastic, and productive.

78. Multi-tasking is not their friend.

While multi-tasking is a common phenomenon today, Trevor notes that autistic people have such intense focus that they work better when focusing on one thing at a time, and being able to either finish a task or come to a good stopping point, rather than going back and forth between two or more tasks. They can be more productive if allowed to work this way.

79. Switching tasks can be very challenging.

Quickly switching tasks is especially difficult for people with autism, especially when it is demanded of them with no notice. This is sometimes unavoidable, but if everyone would consider this a common courtesy—to give notice of a change when possible—the environment would be better for all in the workplace.

80. Interruptions can be hard to handle.

Employers and coworkers should note that people with autism generally don't like to be interrupted, whether it involves giving work responsibilities or making idle chitchat. Trevor didn't usually want to stop his work and make conversation with a coworker, because he felt like he was there only to work and was very focused on that.

81. They need notice about working late.

While autistic people are very good about being on time, they also have more difficulty than others with unexpected overtime work. Exercising courtesy by providing notification as early as possible that there might be a need to stay late will give them time to process the idea and accept it better. This would be appreciated by any employee.

82. Autistic individuals prefer a calm demeanor.

A supervisor who gives orders loudly or abruptly, interrupting the person's task at hand, is especially difficult for people with autism to handle. Trevor said that people like that stressed him out a lot, and he would handle the instructions much better if they were given in a softer tone, without interrupting, when possible.

83. Being blunt is part of autism.

Because of the extra time needed to sort out what they need to say, along with their black and white, literal thinking, autistic people tend to make comments that come out blunt, rude, or simply unusual. Others in the workplace should give them some grace and keep in mind that they don't mean to be rude.

84. Autistic employees can be literal thinkers.

Taking things literally is common with autistic people, and it can lead to misunderstandings. Supervisors should keep this in mind when communicating. Trevor was sometimes taken advantage of and teased by other employees because they found it funny when he took their sarcastic comments seriously.

85. Extra time is needed when new.

Starting a new job is more difficult for autistic people, because anything new and unfamiliar takes them more time and effort to get used to. They need extra time and patience to get the hang of the routine, environment, job duties, and coworkers, and will be working harder than the average employee to adjust.

86. Seeking help is difficult for them.

Some autistic people, including Trevor, tend to be very independent and don't like to ask for help with things they don't understand. It's very important that autistic employees develop the skill of asking for assistance or information while on the job. Supervisors and job coaches can make this easier by checking in and asking if the employee understands his work requirements.

87. Facial expressions can sometimes be deceiving.

People with autism usually have a harder time picking up meanings that are communicated by facial expressions, according to Duncan. Using clear and direct words helps them know what is meant. At the same time, they may not use appropriate facial expressions when they are talking. Asking for clarification is the best way to avoid miscommunication.

88. Face blindness is offensive to some.

Face blindness is the inability to recognize people by their faces at times, especially if they are in a different context, or are dressed differently. This common trait of people with autism can come across as rudeness or forgetfulness, so educating others about face blindness will help alleviate misunderstandings.

89. Social events can be hard work.

While social or morale events in the workplace are a "break" from work for typical workers, they can be hard work for those with autism, Hilbert said. They are often unstructured, and there is an expectation to make small talk. Plus, those with autism don't know what to expect and might feel anxiety about deviating from their routine and possibly falling behind in their planned work duties.

90. Giving advanced notice helps alleviate stress.

The more notice given, the better. Instead of saying, "Hey, it's Jane's birthday, we're all having cake in the break room right now!" the person with autism would prefer to know as soon as possible before the event, even if it's only 30 minutes, so he can finish what he is doing and prepare for the change in routine.

91. Learning about social skills benefits all.

Coworkers can learn to be patient and make an effort to give autistic employees some leeway in social skills that might be lacking. In an ideal workplace, everyone would be treated this way, regardless of whether or not a disability is known. Duncan suggests that employees try to not take things the wrong way, such as when employees with autism decline outings or social gatherings.

Social Expectations for Workers with Autism

92. Learning about social expectations breeds success.

Employees with autism should take it upon themselves to learn as much as possible about workplace social rules, which others pick up on without much effort. There are numerous books that address these situations in detail, such as break room behavior, lunchtimes, morale events, and other any events outside of job duties.

93. Taking short breaks can reduce stress.

Autistic individuals can learn to be in tune with their own unique needs and stressors, and be prepared to do what it takes to still be effective on the job when stressful times happen, says Duncan. This could mean going to the car, taking a break, walking around the building, or whatever helps to de-stress, think, or cool off.

94. Allow time for friendships to grow.

Trevor's supervisor was open to learning about Trevor's needs due to his autism, but Seidler said, "Many people simply don't understand how to interact with people who have autism, and need extra time to build friendships." Autistic people should learn to be patient with other people, and allow time for good working relationships and friendships to develop.

95. Staying clean and groomed is vital.

Following basic hygiene and cleanliness are extremely important for being accepted in the workplace. Although Steve Jobs and others have been successful with odd hygiene habits, it is more likely to be a hindrance to success for an autistic person who already has some differences and challenges at work. Job coaches and books can help in this area.

96. Wear suitable clothing on the job.

Most workplaces have some type of dress code, even if it is unwritten. Learning and following these codes is essential. Employees can also learn by observing other employees, especially those at the same level, to see how closely they follow the rules. Oftentimes dress codes are simply guidelines, and are bent by employees, so violations need not be pointed out.

97. Courtesies and friendly exchanges are protocol.

While greetings are not often important to people with autism, they are an integral part of most jobs. Employees with autism must express basic greetings, such as "Hi," and "How are you?" with coworkers and customers, say "Thank-you," "Please," and "Excuse me," when appropriate, and show respect and courtesy to those around them in the workplace.

98. Small talk is expected at work.

"Professional small talk" (non-work related conversations within the workplace) has appropriate times and places. It is important to learn what to say and how long to continue the conversations among co-workers. Learning body language and other cues will also help the employee fit in to the workday culture. Books and job coaching can help improve these skills.

99. Every workplace has its unique language.

All companies have special terms that refer to anything from departments to job titles. Acronyms are especially prevalent, and even everyday slang and cliches are already challenging for those with autism. Many companies have handouts with acronyms and buzzwords defined. The autistic worker should realize that most new workers are also not comfortable with all terminology, but learning will come in time.

100. Keep searching for the perfect fit.

In closing, please don't give up on finding a job or career that fits you perfectly. There are so many ways to get help and a number of different methods for landing meaningful employment. Some positions won't work out, so try to learn from them, review and adjust your strategies, and try again. I wish you a productive career and a fulfilling life of independence and making a difference in the workplace and in the world.

About the Author

Patty Pacelli is an editor, author, entrepreneur, wife and mother of two adult children, one with an autism spectrum disorder. She promotes autism awareness by serving on the board of directors of the Seattle Children's Autism Guild. She wrote this book to help adults with autism, like her son Trevor, achieve their career dreams and contribute their exceptional talents to the workforce. Patty is also the author of *Six-Word Lessons to Look Your Best.*

Sources Cited

Elaine Duncan, MA, LMHC

Psychotherapist in Autism & EDMR Specialist

Counselingredmond.com

Sara Gardner

Program Manager, Autism Spectrum Navigators

Bellevue College

Bellevuecollege.edu/autismspectrumnavigators

Michael Goodwill

Manager of Transition Services

PROVAIL

Provail.org

Lisa Iland Hilbert, MS

Owner of Social Bridge, LLC

Socialbridgeseattle.com

Jeri Kendle

Social Enterprise Strategist

Southwest Autism Research & Resource Center

Autismcenter.org

Kim Kimbell

Human Resources Consultant

Michael Maloney

Executive Director

Organization for Autism Research

ResearchAutism.org

Paige Morrow

Extraordinary Ventures

Extraordinaryventures.org

Manfred Seidler

Plant Engineer, Crossroads Bible Church

Garry Burge and Ben Wilshire, Adult Asperger's and Autism Advocates

GarryBurge.com

U.S. Department of Labor, public domain, dol.gov.

Najarian, Tamar, "34 Best and 10 Worst Jobs for Adults with Autism" emaxhealth.com.

Danya International (danya.com), Southwest Autism Research & Resource Center (autismcenter.org) and Organization for Autism Research, Mike Maloney, Executive Director, (researchautism.org) *Life Journey Through Autism: A Guide for Transition to Adulthood* (2008)

Roux, Ann M., Shattuck, Paul T., Cooper, Benjamin P., Anderson, Kristy, et al. "Postsecondary Employment Experiences Among Young Adults with an Autism Spectrum Disorder," *Journal of the American Academy of Child & Adolescent Psychiatry*, Volume 52, Issue 9, (2013) 931-939.

For Further Reading and Information

Social Thinking at Work: Why Should I Care?, Michelle Garcia Winner

The Hidden Curriculum: Practical Solutions for Understanding Unstated Rules in Social Situations, Brenda Smith Myles

The Unwritten Rules of Social Relationships: Decoding Social Mysteries through the Unique Perspectives of Autism, Temple Grandin

Six-Word Lessons on Growing Up Autistic, Trevor Pacelli

Six-Word Lessons for Dads with Autistic Kids, Lonnie Pacelli

The Kindergarten Adventures of Amazing Grace, Briana Pacelli

For more resources on autism, go to GrowingUpAutistic.com

Six-Word Lessons for Dads with Autistic Kids

100 Lessons to Help Fathers and their Children Create Strong Bonds

Lonnie Pacelli

GrowingUpAutistic.com

Trevor was born December 1, 1992. By all accounts he appeared to be just like any other baby. His big sister, Briana, is two and one-half years older than Trevor and set the standard for us as to what life with children would be like. At age two Briana was speaking in full sentences, while Trevor at age two was barely saying any words. Briana demanded almost constant attention from my wife, Patty and I, while Trevor preferred to play by himself. Trevor went to speech therapy and then to a special preschool for children with disabilities or behavioral issues. At age five we took him to the University of Washington Autism Center where they tested him and diagnosed him with Autism Spectrum Disorder (ASD) in the category of Pervasive Developmental Disorder – Not Otherwise Specified (PDD-NOS). There it was, we had an autistic child.

As parents we were not at all prepared for life with an ASD child. Patty was a stay-at-home mom and became well versed in how to relate to Trevor; I, not nearly as much as Patty. While I did figure some things out, I made a lot of mistakes as a father that if I got a mulligan would never do again. That's why I wrote Six-Word Lessons for Dads with Autistic Kids.

In Six-Word Lessons for Dads with Autistic Kids, you'll get 100 concise, simple-to-understand lessons written in "man-speak" to help fathers get nuggets quickly and efficiently. Some may apply to your situation, some may not. My hope, though, is you'll be able to implement a few of these nuggets to help you build a stronger bond with your child.

I'd love to hear your thoughts on this book and how any of the lessons have helped or not helped you. Tell us your story at www.growingupautistic.com.

Definitions and Reasons for this Book

1. There are three types of ASDs.

Autism Spectrum Disorders (ASDs) come in three forms: autistic disorder (also known as "classic autism"), Asperger Syndrome, and Pervasive Developmental Disorder – Not Otherwise Specified (PDD-NOS, also known as "atypical autism").

2. Autistic Disorder – the most typical ASD.

Autistic Disorder is what comes to mind when most envision someone with autism. Significant language delays, unusual interests, and social and communication challenges are common. Many also have intellectual disability.

3. Asperger Syndrome – milder Autism Spectrum Disorder.

People with Asperger Syndrome typically have social challenges and unusual, obsessive behaviors and interests. However, they usually do not have intellectual disability or language delay issues.

4. Pervasive Developmental Disorder-Not Otherwise Specified.

People with PDD-NOS often have fewer and milder symptoms than those with Autistic Disorder. Communication and social challenges are generally prevalent.

5. ASDs account for 2% of births

The Center for Disease Control (CDC) estimates are that one in 50 people between the ages of six and seventeen have ASD. This number is up from one in 88 surveyed in 2007.

6. Boys have ASD more than girls.

According to an extensive CDC study conducted in 2008, boys are five times more likely than girls to have Autism Spectrum Disorder.

7. There's no one cause of ASD.

Some potential causes linked to ASD are having a sibling or parent with ASD, taking thalidomide or valproic acid during pregnancy and some genetic disorders. There is no one definitive cause as to why someone is born with ASD.

8. Unproven causes of Autism Spectrum Disorder.

Vaccines, tantrums, junk food, bad parenting, television, stressful family situations, or cell phones have not been reliably proven to cause ASD. While there may be other results from these factors, ASD has not been proven to be linked to any of them.

9. The lessons you'll be reading about.

The experiences you will read in the rest of this book apply predominantly to those with PDD-NOS and Asperger's, as this is where our first-hand parental experience with ASD lies. However, many of the lessons included will apply to those with autistic disorder as well. My hope is you pick up several nuggets to help you in your journey as the father of an ASD child.

10. The people you'll be reading about.

There are three people I will refer to in this book. Patty is my wonderful wife and is very active in ASD awareness. Briana is our eldest and is a nurse. Trevor is our youngest and desires a career in film. Trevor was diagnosed with PDD-NOS at age five. The experiences you'll read about revolve around us as a family and our journey with ASD.

11. I screwed up way too much.

I didn't write this book because I did everything right in being a father to Trevor. In fact, I did a lot of things wrong in my parenting. I wasn't nearly as sensitive as I needed to be when it came to accommodating a child with ASD. My one goal is to help other fathers of an ASD child avoid some of the same mistakes I made.

Cues your Child May Have ASD

12. They may have very obsessive interests.

From very early on, Trevor showed obsessive interests in certain things. At age two it was puzzles. At age five it was the television show *Blues Clues*. Throughout his childhood he was obsessed with drawing just about anything. He still has strong interests such as movies (fortunately that is his chosen profession) but is not nearly as obsessive as when he was younger.

13. They just want to be alone.

Many with ASD are perfectly content being on their own, focused on their favorite activities. This can be perplexing, particularly when the autistic child has siblings who like interaction. Briana was a very social child who craved interaction. Trevor was the polar opposite. As an adult he still needs his alone time.

14. They avoid looking into your eyes.

Those with ASD typically avoid eye contact. With Trevor, we found that it wasn't that he disliked eye contact, it was just something he didn't normally do. Patty and I consciously worked with him to look us in the eye when talking. As an adult he mostly establishes and engages in eye contact during conversations.

15. They have difficulty expressing their feelings.

Many with ASD have difficulty verbalizing feelings of happiness, sadness, anger, etc. You can definitely see through their actions how they are feeling, but they are less likely to verbalize it. Trevor as an adult still has difficulty with this at times and gets frustrated with himself when he can't verbalize his feelings.

16. They don't read other people well.

Because those with ASD are so into their own world and are very literal by nature, they have difficulty "reading" other people and observing social cues like facial expressions, moods, or tone of voice. Trevor had a lot of difficulty with this growing up but has grown more aware of social cues as an adult. For example, he now understands sarcasm and will say, "That's sarcasm right?"

17. They have peculiar repetitive body movements.

Some with ASD may flap their hands, run in circles, or do some other body movement. Trevor would rock from side to side in bed before going to sleep. This started with birth and continued into his early elementary years. He would also run in circles in the living room and talk to himself, which seemed to calm him.

18. They need to keep a schedule.

Having the ability to keep to a schedule is important to someone with ASD. You could set your watch to some things Trevor did during the day, like setting the dinner table

(5:50 p.m.), walking on the treadmill (6:30 p.m.), or having an evening snack (8:00 p.m.). We consequently kept a very orderly and predictable house and all four of us grew very comfortable with schedules.

19. Even fun surprises can wreak havoc.

So what kid doesn't like hearing, "Hey, let's go out for ice cream!" While many kids would gleefully run for the car, those with ASD could find it difficult because it is an unplanned activity that wasn't expected. We learned to not spring unplanned activities of any kind on Trevor; we would give him advance notice so he could incorporate the activity into his schedule.

20. Trying new things isn't very fun.

Whether it be new foods, new activities, or different clothes, doing something new takes the person with ASD out of his familiar routine and disrupts his plans. With food, we had an agreement with Trevor that he had to try something ten times before he decided he didn't like it. Had we not done this, he might still be eating hot dogs, grilled cheese, or macaroni and cheese for nearly every meal.

21. They have delayed speech and language.

Those with ASD typically lag in speech and language progression. When Trevor was two years old he was barely saying 10 words, which was a stark contrast to Briana, who was rifling off entire sentences by age two. His comprehension was also delayed. He began private speech and language therapy at age two to help him interact using words.

22. Their senses are much more sensitive.

Senses such as smells, sounds, and touch are more sensitive in people with ASD, and they can be much more amplified, causing sometimes severe and unusual reactions. Trevor is sensitive to loud noises, and in elementary school he wore headphones at events such as school assemblies to drown out the high noise levels. As an adult, he is more tolerant, but still gets agitated at unexpected or sudden loud noises.

Will He Ever Amount to Anything?

23. What is your definition of "anything"?

As fathers, we innately have visions of our newborn children being the next Einstein, Lincoln, or Gehrig. Discovering your child has ASD can feel like cold water being thrown on your expectations. Raising a child with ASD means being more open to what success will look like for your child and realigning your expectations of him.

24. Will he be able to drive?

While some people with ASD do not learn to drive, many are actually excellent drivers. Trevor had difficulty with the written test, so he was allowed to take the test with audio headphones as well as the usual video, which helped him to pass. He passed the driving portion on the first try and got his license at 16. His driving instructor's only criticism was that he sometimes, "drove too slow." That would be music to any parent's ears!

25. Can he take care of himself?

From the time he was a toddler, we let Trevor do as much as possible for himself, such as dressing and making breakfast, just as we did with Briana. He was probably ahead of the average child in many areas, and always loved being independent. We gave him instruction where needed, but always expected him to do things for himself. This served him well as he grew up and he is now living on his own in a college residence hall.

26. Will he get married some day?

Many with ASD are happily married and have found the perfect mate to share their life with. Trevor has the desire to be married someday but is not preoccupied with the notion. He is more focused on working toward a successful career in the film industry.

27. Will his children also have ASD?

Given that there is one no clear cause of ASD, it's difficult to say whether or not a parent with ASD will have children with ASD. One of Trevor's teachers in college has Asperger's and has a child with Asperger's and one non-ASD child. The more important question is whether your child wants and is capable of being a parent; not whether your child will have a child with ASD.

28. Will he ever have any friends?

Making friends was certainly one of Trevor's major challenges growing up. Up until he was in ninth grade, he had a few casual friends, but didn't have a strong desire to make or have friends. The older he got, the more he wanted friends, but it was always difficult to form those friendships. He still struggles in this area, but has made great strides at learning skills and making the effort to make and maintain friendships.

29. Will kids make fun of him?

This was very painful for us. Yes, other kids did make fun of Trevor and knew what buttons to push to get him agitated. Others who he thought were friends turned out to be mean kids who took advantage of his ASD. He saw a therapist during high school to help him with some of his struggles.

30. Will he ever have a job?

Having ASD doesn't mean your child will be forever unable to work. Trevor got his first job after high school working at a summer camp. He subsequently worked at our church doing maintenance work while in college. We were amazed at what he was able to do and his employers loved his promptness, willingness to do any job, and his being "all business" when at work.

31. Will he always need our help?

When we compare Trevor's with Briana's "neediness indexes," both still need us for different things. Trevor needs a bit more coaching on new life skills events, such as signing up for college classes for the first time. We are very deliberate in establishing our parental role as coaches and tell him, "Our job is to tell you what we think, your job is to decide what to do with it."

My Spouse and I Don't Agree

32. One knows more than the other.

It's likely that one of you will have done more research on ASDs and techniques to use in parenting your child. It's super important you both get well versed on the basics of ASDs (this book is a good start), that you do some of your own research, and you recommend reading to each other to help you get up to speed.

33. One doesn't believe he has ASD.

I've met a number of parents where one spouse was in denial about an ASD diagnosis for their child. This is quite simply a recipe for disaster. If necessary, get a second opinion but be proactive in taking steps to ensure you both align on the ASD diagnosis.

34. One is overprotective and shelters him.

In our experience, it has been good to have some healthy tension, with Patty being more protective and me wanting Trevor to fend for himself. Either one of us working alone might have erred to one extreme or the other. If you differ in this area, embrace the difference and look for common ground.

35. One wants to make him normal.

At the writing of this book there is no known cure for any of the Autism Spectrum Disorders. You have to work together based on a goal of supporting your child with ASD, not trying to cure him of it. You'll have much greater success if you adopt a mindset of acceptance.

36. One doesn't want to be involved.

In my opinion, having one parent shoulder the full weight of caring for and nurturing an ASD child while the other plays the role of non-existent parent is worse than a single person raising an ASD child on his or her own. The involved parent has enough on his or her plate without having to deal with an apathetic spouse. If there are two parents, ensure both are involved.

37. Grandparents have different points of view.

You may have parents who feel obligated to give their opinion on how you should be raising your ASD child. Watch out for conflicting or uninformed opinions which drive a wedge between you and your spouse, particularly if there is no prior experience with ASD. Accept their opinion then together with your spouse decide what to do with it.

Why Doesn't He Like Normal Things?

38. Beware some sports will frustrate him.

We signed Trevor up for soccer when he was four. When on the field he would stand there and cry. What we learned was that the randomness of play and the yelling by parents and other kids was too much for him to take. We found more orderly sports like baseball and tennis to be more palatable to him, though he was never really passionate about either playing or watching sports.

39. Vacations can throw him off schedule.

On our first day at Walt Disney World, Trevor told us at 3 p.m. that we needed to go back to the hotel room so he could watch *Blues Clues*. We were in a place all kids love, but he didn't want to break his routine. As he got older we convinced him that when we were on vacation there was no routine, so his "vacation" routine was that everything would be different, which he was OK with.

40. Recess isn't all fun and games.

Because Trevor craves order in his life, the randomness, yelling and other activity at recess was frustrating for him. While other kids may love the activity and stimulation, a child with ASD may very well see it as stressful and confusing.

41. Surprises aren't such a good idea.

Some people with ASD can be so lost in their own world that they are incredibly sensitive to anything unexpected. Surprises such as sneaking behind their back to intentionally startle them or other teasing usually upsets them.

42. He really needs some time alone.

Briana loves being around people most of the time. Being around people for extended periods of time gets exhausting for Trevor. Even around family members or people he likes, he needs to have time to get away by himself. In college Trevor was able to get a private dorm room so he could safely retreat to a place he always knew he could be alone.

43. What kid doesn't like drinking soda?

The first time Trevor took a sip of soda he puked all over the table (and of course we were in a restaurant). He also didn't eat his first cheeseburger until he was nine. Some foods that most kids love might not appeal to a child with ASD.

44. Joking can be no laughing matter.

Because people with ASD have difficulty discerning between seriousness and joking, some may be confused, offended, or hurt by what may seem to be a harmless joke. As Trevor has gotten older he's been better about jokes, but still gets hurt if a joke is directed at him.

45. Hugs can be uncomfortable or painful.

With his heightened sensitivity to touch, Trevor didn't particularly enjoy being hugged as a toddler or adolescent. Over time, he has learned that hugging is an acceptable social norm. As an adult, if we don't see him for more than a couple of days Trevor will gladly give us a brief hug along with a big "Hi!"

46. Sleepovers weren't very fun for him.

Sleepovers (either staying at another house or having a friend over) meant a change in routine and not being able to do the things Trevor typically got to do on his own. When he did stay at another house for the night we gave him plenty of warning and ensured he had time by himself to avoid getting frustrated with too many people around.

47. He can't explain what's bothering him.

Trevor may have something that is bothering him, but at times he finds it difficult to put his feelings into words. If Patty or I ask him what's wrong, sometimes he'll tell us that something is wrong but he doesn't know how to put it into words.

Helping with Reading, Writing, and Arithmetic

48. To homeschool or not to homeschool.

Patty and I decided to partially homeschool Trevor for seventh and eighth grades, then he returned to public school from ninth grade on. Homeschooling was helpful because it gave him more focused help than he would have received in public school. The downside was that he didn't get as much social interaction. Looking back, we believe we made the right decision to homeschool for those crucial years.

49. What were your strongest school subjects?

My stronger subjects were math and science, while Patty's were language arts and humanities. We divvied up homework and homeschool responsibilities by those topic areas to give Trevor the best quality of education and homework assistance. He also attended a homeschool learning center part-time, which was a valuable support.

50. Don't force your strengths on him.

While math and science were my stronger suit, I was dealing with a child who didn't enjoy either of those topics. Trevor and I would both get frustrated with each other when he wasn't getting something that I thought he should be getting. I wanted him to do well in those subjects because I did well in those subjects. Man was I wrong.

51. Professional tutors can help big time.

Trevor was fortunate enough to have some dedicated tutoring assistance in a couple of his classes. This was tremendous in that it wasn't mom or dad doing the tutoring and the tutor was much closer to the content and learning methods being used in school. It was extremely helpful.

52. What is an IEP all about?

In the United States the Individuals with Disabilities Education Act (IDEA) mandates that children with disabilities be put on an Individualized Education Plan (IEP). Some may see this as bureaucracy at work; I saw it as a great way to partner with the school to ensure the best possible instruction. You must know about your child's IEP and be actively involved in its execution.

53. Encourage involvement in social groups.

Trevor has always loved the arts and in middle school joined the drama club, which continued through high school. He was involved both onstage as a performer and offstage doing various jobs such as props and set decoration. His experience in drama was significant in helping him shape his social skills and learn how to interact with peers.

54. Partner with the teachers and administrators.

We learned early on that having a regular dialogue with Trevor's teachers, counselors, and administrators was huge in helping to ensure the best possible learning experience which would lead to Trevor's success. Even during our two years of homeschooling, we utilized the public school system for courses, counseling, speech therapy, and IEP assistance.

55. Be aware of the potential bully.

It's no joke that kids can be mean, and an ASD child can be even more susceptible to bullying. As a parent, it's important to work actively with the school system on any bullying incidents and to reinforce with your child that he has done nothing wrong if innocent. He already is likely feeling angry over the incident; you'll make it worse if you are anything less than supportive with him.

56. Accommodations don't stop after high school.

Trevor went to a community college for two years after high school. We saw that as a great stepping stone for him. The college has a very active ASD support program headed by a director with Asperger's. He then transferred to a four-year university with an active disability resource center where he was allowed accommodations such as a private dorm room and ability to take tests in a room by himself.

Disciplining Can Have Very Unintended Consequences

57. Don't ever discipline out of anger.

Sure, this is something a parent should practice with any child. With Trevor, whenever I would get angry with him, any negative feelings he had would be amplified and replayed over and over in his mind. It affected him much more than it did Briana and he still can vividly recall whenever I was angry at him. This one I'll regret for the rest of my life.

58. He must know when he's wrong.

Regardless of ASD, the child must learn right from wrong to the extent he is capable of understanding, and recognize there are consequences when misbehaving. Be careful about being too accommodating and not correcting wrong behavior because of his ASD.

59. Alignment with your spouse is crucial.

Patty and I weren't always aligned when it came to disciplining either Briana or Trevor. This not only created stress with the kids, it created stress between us. Be deliberate about putting a discipline game plan together and stick with it.

60. Raising your voice exacerbates the problem.

I came from a family of yellers who would raise their voices when angry. Because of this, the idea of raising one's voice when disciplining seemed natural to me, so that's what I did. For Trevor, raising my voice coupled with his sensitivity to sound was like nails on a blackboard to him. It was not the right method and didn't help at all.

61. Find ways to discipline without agitating.

We used a couple of techniques which worked well. One was losing a privilege, such as their usual bedtime reading and music cassettes (my kids remember this as "no book and no tape"). The other was getting "work chips" where they got a poker chip which represented an extra household task like emptying the dishwasher. Both worked well to get the point across.

62. Don't show favorites when disciplining them.

When siblings are in the picture, be careful not to let your child with ASD get away with some things that the siblings would not get away with. The siblings will sniff out the unfairness in discipline and be resentful of the child with ASD. At the same time, the child with ASD may also see that he can get away with more things and take advantage of you.

63. Being blunt isn't reason to discipline.

Many people with ASD are extremely blunt and direct in their conversation. With Trevor, I characterize it as, "Trevor just says what everyone else is thinking or wants to say." While he might have come across as rude, he wasn't misbehaving--it's simply how he's naturally wired. Use those times as calm teaching moments to help him learn and not as opportunities to discipline.

64. Tell him that you love him.

Disciplining can be confusing for any child, especially when disciplining out of anger. For a child with ASD, the feelings get amplified and he can take any discipline as a sign that he is a bad person or that you hate him. Make sure he knows you love him and that discipline is about correcting behavior, not about withholding love.

He's Not You, Get Over it

65. You live yours, he lives his.

First and foremost, you need to accept and embrace that your ASD child may be interested in much, some, or none of what you are interested in. You may have envisioned your child being a star sports figure, a power CEO, or a famous actor. That's all really nice, but it doesn't matter. As with any child, he needs to discover and follow his own passion.

66. But I see so much potential!

True, there might be the potential for your ASD child to do something great. Force it on him and you're sure to cause him to run the other way. It could just be that his passion needs to grow into his potential. Give him time and space to do it.

67. How about we watch some football?

I can make this statement and get an immediate "Sure, Dad!", but it comes from Briana. She'll watch game after game with me. Trevor has no interest in watching football or any kind of sports with me. As much as I'd like for both my kids to watch football, I am very content with the other activities Trevor and I enjoy together, like watching movies and eating at Old Country Buffet.

68. Maybe he'll follow me into business.

I love business and the challenge of creating something that others want and will pay for. Trevor loves creating things, but not for profit motive. He loves the artistic side of creating things and couldn't care less about the "business" side of things. He's not passionate about it and probably never will be.

69. I walked five miles to school…

Every father has stories about how his kids have life so much easier than he did. While it's good to remind your ASD child of the luxuries that he has in life, it's not cool to make him feel guilty about it. Remember people with ASD tend to amplify things, so what may seem minor to you could be like the end of the world to him.

70. Tell him how you've messed up.

Trevor loves to hear that his dad is human, that he's made mistakes, and that he's willing to admit his mistakes to his son. A number of times when talking through a mistake Trevor has made I'll tell him a story of how I really screwed something up. He loves to hear that his old man has done some dumb stuff (correction: a lot of dumb stuff) and that I'm willing to admit it to him. It's very therapeutic for both of us.

71. Remind him of his own strengths.

Trevor likes it when I praise strengths particularly when his strengths are my weaknesses, for example, his drawing skill. When he was younger, we would play a restaurant game while waiting for dinner. I would ask him to draw what the baby would look like if two characters (say Goofy and Minnie) got married and had a baby. The drawings were amazing. I on the other hand can't even draw stick figures.

Find Things to Get Interested In

72. What TV shows does he watch?

With Trevor, it was easy to know which TV shows he liked to watch. He talked about them. We started watching a few TV shows together and took to recording them so we could watch them right after dinner. It gave us an opportunity to talk about the TV show and weave in other conversations around the show.

73. What movies are interesting to him?

Men in Black. Trevor and I both love that movie and have seen it dozens of times. We also did quite a few visits to the theater to see movies. Some were great, some not so great. The point is that going to and watching movies is something that he and I do together and has helped in our bonding as father and son.

74. Does he talk about any hobbies?

With an ASD child it is usually pretty easy to hone in on his interests. He'll do it all the time and/or talk about it constantly. Watch to see what things he is interested in and do some parallel play together, then use it as a means to talk about things with him.

75. Favorite restaurants help with creating bonds.

Growing up, Trevor had some favorite places to eat. When he was a toddler it was McDonalds. Later it became Old Country Buffet, now it's The Melting Pot. We also enjoy going to breakfast together and now whenever we're with my father-in-law he expects that we're going to go out to breakfast together. It's just part of the routine.

76. Make sure it becomes scheduled time.

Trevor's and my special activities are almost always scheduled in some way. For things we would do on a regular basis we would have a set time that we would do it. For special events, it worked best to give him advance notice so he could plan it into his schedule. Don't spring an activity on him last minute, even if it's something he loves to do.

77. Don't interfere with spouse and child.

There are some things that Trevor and I do together, and there are some things that Trevor and Patty do together. Trevor enjoys those times and prefers that Patty and I don't infringe on the other's special time.

78. Be mindful of competing with him.

Trevor is very interested in photography and has an incredible eye for finding amazing shots. I am very supportive of his hobby and genuinely am amazed at his photographic prowess. He wants it to be his thing and doesn't want me to go out and buy a camera and take pictures with him. We're completely content going somewhere where he can take great pictures and I watch him at his craft.

79. Parallel play can be very effective.

Trevor and I had a kids game that we would play on the internet where Flintstones characters would do things like have snowball fights. He and I played that game together but did it on two separate computers sitting side by side playing our own games. It was a lot of fun because we got to talk a lot about how we were doing in the game but we also were playing separately.

80. Interact but let him stay focused.

Doing things together means participating in an activity while at the same time sprinkling in conversation and questions. His being engrossed in an activity is like studying for a final; he's very focused on what he's doing and constant interruption is likely to agitate him. Don't overpower him with interaction.

Get Him to Try New Things

81. You need to help him grow.

Because people with ASD seek comfort in routine, they need help being introduced to new experiences. As a child, Trevor played so well independently that it was easy to just let him do his thing because he was content. However, he needed to grow and develop new routines and interests otherwise he'd stay stuck in neutral.

82. We used a "ten times" technique.

Getting Trevor to try new foods was very difficult. Popcorn, hot dogs, milk, and macaroni and cheese were among his few favorites. Whenever he would try new food, his immediate reaction was that he didn't like it. We used a "ten times" technique where he had to try something ten times before he decided he didn't like it. We weren't militant about enforcement, but it did get him to try new foods and broaden his menu.

83. Let him create routine around it.

Creating a routine around trying new things helps to put something familiar and predictable around something that is not familiar and predictable. Setting an expectation such as, "on Thursdays after dinner we're going to do something we haven't done before" allows him to schedule it in his day and prepare himself for the new activity.

84. Be patient when introducing new things.

As fathers, we tend to want to fix things like repairing a leaky faucet. If you're like me, you also want to see results quickly and feel like, "If I do more then I'll see results faster." Not true with your ASD child. You've got to be patient and not flood him with new things looking for quick results. This is a marathon; you can't run it like a 100-yard dash.

85. Not every new thing will stick.

Just like you may not enjoy every new thing that is sprung on you, don't expect that every new thing you introduce to your child is going to stick. If he's just not interested in the activity after trying it a few times then move on and look for something else to introduce. Remember he's not you; just because you may like something doesn't mean he'll like it.

86. Use numbers when trying new things.

Using a numeric goal worked well with Trevor. Setting a goal like "learn one new thing this summer" and choosing a specific task, made it black and white to him and something he could easily understand. This is much more meaningful than saying, "Try some new things this summer."

87. Work together when introducing new things.

Riding a two-wheeler was a huge accomplishment for Trevor. As a young teenager he still didn't know how to ride a bike, so I was more of the goal-setter of getting him to learn to ride a bike by end of summer and Patty was the teacher who worked with him every day. Her softer style was much more conducive to his learning ability. He did learn to ride and grew to really enjoy it, even riding to school.

Don't Underestimate His Life Skills Abilities

88. He learned to drive a car.

Trevor and Patty practiced driving for hours and hours at school parking lots and in our neighborhood. We also signed Trevor up for private driving lessons to help give him any special attention needed to improve his driving skills. After one of his early driving classes he noticed that our license plate tabs were expired on one of our cars. He not only learned to drive well but saved us a ticket in the process!

89. He manages his own bank account.

When Trevor was 16 we got him a checking account with a debit card and worked with him on the fundamentals of how to use an ATM, how to write a check, and how to check his balance online. His account was linked to ours so we could also monitor what was happening and look for any abnormalities.

90. He uses a credit card responsibly.

When Trevor was 18 we signed him up for a credit card, explained how to use it, including paying his bill online. We explained that he would need to pay it off every month or would start incurring interest charges. We also linked this account to ours to monitor activity. He's never missed a due date and hasn't paid a dime in interest.

91. He made the college dean's list.

Trevor has been on the dean's list multiple times and has had several quarters where he got all A's in his classes. We saw a big jump in his grades once he learned how to more effectively study by rewriting his notes. The visual and physical action of rewriting notes helped him to better retain information and do better in school.

92. He had chores around the house.

From the time Briana and Trevor were little we gave them chores to do. Trevor had to clean his room and vacuum the stairs. He created a routine of doing them every Sunday around 2:30. Once when Patty's parents were watching the kids for a weekend they were amazed how on Sunday afternoon the kids both did their chores without being asked. Routine has its benefits!

93. He completely takes care of himself.

Now that he is living away from home, Trevor shops for himself, studies on his own, finds his way around, and calls us when he needs help with something. Patty and I instilled self-sufficiency in both Briana and Trevor early in life so he really knows no other way than to take care of himself.

Remember You Have Other Kids Too

94. Make it just something you do.

At home we kept a consistent schedule to create more predictability. For example, we ate dinner at 6:00 every night at the table with no TV or other distractions. It not only helped with predictability but was tremendous for building relationships and keeping in touch with the kids through their teens. Patty and I still dine at 6:00.

95. Do special things with each child.

Briana and I had special traditions that only she and I did. Every Memorial Day weekend, we would do a six-mile walk together. Every Christmas Eve we would shop for a Northwest seafood dinner that the family would eat after church that night. Now that she's an adult, I am so thankful we did those daddy-daughter things. They have definitely helped build a strong relationship.

96. Rotate responsibilities with each of them.

At bedtime, Patty and I would rotate who would put which child to bed each night. The kids got to spend dedicated time with each of us during their bedtime routine. Briana and I had our little things only she and I would do, like reading Ranger Rick magazine at bedtime.

97. Do things with all of them.

We all four love watching movies and can quote lines from movies such as How the Grinch Stole Christmas ("Stay Focused!"), Mrs. Doubtfire ("Hellllooooooo!"), Aladdin ("BEEEE Yourself!") and A Christmas Story (Fra-GEE-lay!). Now that the kids are adults, they still love to rattle off movie lines. We love it too.

The Journey Doesn't End, it Changes

98. Provide a safe environment for advice.

The evening we left Trevor at his dorm room we had a discussion over dinner about soliciting advice. We told him, "For small decisions, get advice from one person you trust, for big decisions, get advice from three people you trust." Four weeks later he asked our advice about something. We gave it to him and he said, "See I had a small decision and asked your advice." Loved it.

99. Leverage your job as a coach.

We have been very deliberate with Trevor about letting him know that Patty and I are now planning to do less parenting and more coaching with him. This reinforces a number of concepts: he is an adult and is responsible for his own decisions; we are there for him; he gets to decide what advice to take; and he is accountable for the outcome of his decisions.

100. Never stop saying I love you.

Some fathers have difficulty expressing this to anyone, especially their kids. Every time we talk with Trevor or Briana I make it a point to tell them that we love them very much. It's not only important for them to hear it, it's important for me to say it and remind myself what a wonderful son and daughter we've been blessed with.

Citations

Lessons 1-8 – Center for Disease Control http://www.cdc.gov/ncbddd/autism/

Six Word Lessons on Growing Up Autistic

100 Lessons to Understand How Autistic People See Life

Trevor Pacelli

GrowingUpAutistic.com

One percent of the population of children in the U.S. aged 3-17 have an autism spectrum disorder…

One in 68 newborns in the U.S. will be born with an autism spectrum disorder…

Only 56% of students with autism finish high school…

One million Americans live with an autism spectrum disorder…

My name is Trevor Pacelli. I was diagnosed with Autism at age 5. I am the first in my extended family to have autism. Growing up autistic has been difficult not only for me but for my parents and my sister. We've all had to learn about autism and how to maintain a peaceful household. I deeply want other families with autistic children to learn from my experiences. This is why I wrote *Six Word Lessons on Growing Up Autistic.*

In this book you will find 100 short, practical tips to help understand the autistic person in your life, told through insightful personal experiences by someone who has grown up autistic. Rather than pore through pages and pages of content, *Six-Word Lessons on Growing Up Autistic* gives them to you quickly and easily.

My hope is that you are able to use my experiences to help you with raising your autistic child, or relating to anyone you know who is living with autism. Tell me how it's impacted you at story@6wordlessons.com.

For my sister, Briana, for understanding me when no one else did.

For my Mom, Patty, for helping me write and edit this book.

For my Dad, Lonnie, for encouraging me to write this book.

And for my Auntie Lori, who is now with her Savior.

.

Suspecting that your Child has Autism

1. Other children don't act like yours.

Some first clues that a child has autism are the differences from other children. A few of these clues are: delayed speech, not under-standing what you are communicating, crying when held, advanced abilities and obsession in a specific area, such as, for me, putting together puzzles.

2. The doctor has the right voice.

"I'm sorry to tell you this, but your child has autism." It's scary to hear this coming from the doctor when your child is first diagnosed. Your pediatrician is a good first step for finding specialists who will help with a diagnosis. The doctors should be honest, even if it contradicts what you want to hear, or what your friends are telling you

3. Some don't like to be hugged.

Children with autism like to have their space, and that means they sometimes dislike having people in physical contact with them. Although it's not true in my case, many autistic children feel very strongly about being held, touched, or hugged.

4. Speech is an important early sign.

According to my pediatrician, by age two, a child should be speaking at least two words to form an idea. If not, this is a good reason to suspect autism. This was the case with me, and I immediately began work with a speech and language pathologist, to help me learn to comprehend as well as communicate better.

5. Do they ever make eye contact?

Children with autism are often more interested in the texture of the furniture than they are in you, so they may not make eye contact with you. However, they are very observant, so they will notice everything, including your attitude toward them.

6. A child's mannerisms are quite distinguishable.

Does she sway when she walks? Is her posture leaning a certain direction? An autistic child can have physical habits that make her stand out. These habits can be managed with physical or occupational therapy. I appreciated it when people kept in mind that it was still part of my identity.

7. They may interact differently with siblings.

Most parents have multiple children, and when they are young, the kids are together much of the time. If one of them has autism, he may have a more difficult time getting along with his siblings. Work with his siblings to help them understand your autistic child's differences and needs, especially for time alone.

8. They very rarely share their thoughts.

You may think they are being secretive and simply not sharing. But I have this issue all the time as well, and I can say that usually these children are just really protective over what fantasies go on in their head.

9. They don't like to be disturbed.

Because autistic children are not very open with their thoughts in the real world, they can't stand when people try to break the barriers in their heads. Until they learn better coping skills, they will most likely cry, scream and get upset with their parents when interrupted.

10. New places often make them cry.

Leaving the house for a new place can intimidate autistic children. Because they are not familiar with anything, they will complain about wanting to go home. To prepare for this, bring something like a favorite toy, and give plenty of advance details about the outing.

11. They play very well by themselves.

My mom tells me that I was actually easy to take care of when I was very young, because I loved playing by myself. I could stay focused on my favorite activity, puzzles, for hours, and didn't need any attention. This was very different from my sister, who demanded a lot of interaction from a parent or other child.

A Different View of the World

12. You won't believe what they think.

Most people think in logical terms, others think in imaginative terms. But some who have autism, such as myself, think in completely abstract terms that makes little sense to others. It is a combination of imagination and how they see things.

13. They don't just see a tree.

Instead of just seeing a tree, they may add on to that and imagine it painted pink and yellow, sprouting seventeen eyeballs and growing to Godzilla height. Their imagi-nation lets them see everything as a world of their own.

14. Their imagination is over the top.

A grapefruit peels open and a hybrid giraffe-bat comes out and sings Mary Had a Little Lamb in Chinese. That is just an example of how my imagination functions. Anyone other than me would not understand where I got this.

15. They observe everything to the extreme.

With my case of autism, I have a very strong attention to detail, for I notice little things that other people do not. Others like me also have this, and it has been shown that most autistic people are extremely visual learners and observers.

16. They find it tough to explain.

With all that is happening in my head, I sometimes cannot find it in me to share any of it with others. My thoughts are very personal to me, and I usually just can't form thoughts into words.

17. Only focus on one single subject.

Because I get so focused and absorbed into whatever I am doing, it often takes a full hour to fully move on from that activity to another. This is one reason transitions are one of the most common difficulties for autistic people.

18. It's difficult to try new activities.

I have certain subjects, such as drawing and art, in which I'm very fascinated. When I was younger, I actually had an aversion to any other subjects or interests that were not my own, and often did not want to join in such activities.

19. Are exceptionally talented in their areas

With myself, I know that I have a true gift in drawing and photography. Every autistic child is not artistic, but they usually have a specific exceptional talent that stands out. One may be a whiz in history, a master in marine biology, or even a careful nutritionist!

20. They get either As or Fs.

With some autistic kids, their brains allow them to do either tremendously well or horribly. One may be a master in science and just breeze through all the labs, but just cannot perform a math equation to save his life.

21. Nobody on earth thinks like them.

I have met very few people who have the same wide-ranged, detailed thinking style that I possess. Every individual who has autism has a unique way of thinking, which can provide help in areas that no one else can.

Time Alone Versus Time with Others

22. Most autistic kids need time alone.

I have always felt that having time by myself helps me to unwind and smell the petunias. But this doesn't mean I'm antisocial. I still enjoy the company of friends and family, just not as much as most people.

23. Some actually prefer to be alone.

While I do not necessarily always want to be alone, I still feel much more sustainable with myself and able to unleash my emotions when I'm on my own. Others who are like me may also feel happier when alone.

24. Balance solo activities with parental interaction.

While it was easy for my parents to leave me alone to play when I was young, part of my speech and language therapy was for them to actually play with me and talk to me in specific ways that taught me to communicate better. It just needs to be balanced with the needed time alone.

25. They also want to go out.

In high school, even though I needed time alone, hanging out with people outside of school was my main desire. I felt very envious whenever I saw my friends hang out with others and felt a powerful urge to fit in with everyone else.

26. They need to vent their problems

Some may have to explain what's troubling them immediately to others. But it has always been important to me to have some time alone for a while to reflect over what is bothering me before expressing it verbally.

27. Getting out helps their social skills.

I can name times I have been out with friends and said things that have hurt someone's feelings. But getting out and being with friends helped me to be more aware of other people's reactions and emotions.

28. Everyone needs to be socially active.

If everybody avoided socializing and never left their house, then the world would be a terribly boring place! Every human who has ever lived--even those with autism--has his piece to fill in this giant puzzle known as society.

29. Some can have sudden mood swings.

One minute, they love talking to others. Then suddenly, a painful memory comes up in their heads and they no longer want to speak. I always have this happen to me and it certainly affects how I react around others.

30. They can function properly when alone.

Whenever I am by myself, I feel like I can think more about whatever is going on in my life. If I am around a huge crowd for an extended period of time, I can't properly process all the overwhelming activity.

31. On vacation, they need alone time.

For any age, whenever visiting relatives, sightseeing, or going out for extended periods of time, they need time away from others to be on their own. I still feel the need for occasional times alone while I'm out on vacation.

Sudden Changes are a Big Challenge

32. Beware of them throwing a fit.

When I was much younger, I often cried and fell to the ground every time something unexpected happened. Even if it was a trip to the zoo--something kids would usually be excited about-- I felt really strongly about it because it wasn't expected.

33. They plan out their entire day.

I personally function best when I plan my day, which means planning what I am going to do and for how long. This is why I feel so strongly about sudden plans that interfere with my schedule throughout the day.

34. They can't transition between things easily.

As I have said, it is difficult for me to move from one activity to the next. I can only make a smooth transition in a proper setting that accommodates what I'm doing along with enough support to push me through.

35. Their brains need time to process.

Although I am better now with sudden schedule changes, I still need some time to process the thought before I can go along with the change. That's really all that most autistic kids need to calm them down: time.

36. Reactions can come out as unexpected.

You say to your autistic child, "We're going to the park to play Frisbee!" but your child may just cry and whine. Although they usually love going to the park, they just weren't ready to go right at that minute.

37. They like to set a schedule.

I always wake up at a certain time, shower at a certain time, and have a set time to go to sleep every day. I rarely go out of this routine and this really helps to keep my mind stable.

38. They dislike not getting their way.

It's not necessarily, "my way or the highway," but rather, "I was ready to have this happen to me, not something else." I'm so ready for one thing to occur that when the opposite happens, I become unhappy.

39. Learning new things is really hard.

For those who have autism, it can take at least twice as long or more to learn something new. They are not used to anything unfamiliar, and don't really want to feel forced to apply something new to their life.

40. Surprises aren't such a good idea.

One thing about people with autism is that they can be so lost in their own little world that they are incredibly sensitive to anything unexpected. Surprises such as sneaking behind their back to intentionally startle them or other teasing usually upsets them.

41. Just think patterns. Just think patterns.

My daily life follows a pattern: Get up, go to class, go home, do homework, and go to bed. Anyone with autism would follow a similar pattern. Once the parent notices this as well, they will better understand the child.

Getting Out There to Make Friends

42. Time with friends versus time alone.

Everybody has to get out there and be social with people, right? But if someone has autism--at any age--they need to learn to balance needed and desired friendships with time alone, which I need to unleash my emotions and unwind from the worldly pressures.

43. They don't know what to say.

Some people with autism have difficulty forming into words what exactly they are trying to tell someone. I still have this issue. The idea is in my head perfectly, but forming it into words is difficult and takes time.

44. Getting to know people is difficult.

I can clearly say that for autistic people, it is really hard to find something they have in common with others. Since their attention is not fully on the person, they don't know what to say or do while around them.

45. They can't explain what's bothering them.

Again, people with autism don't know how to explain their thoughts. If you ask them what's bothering them, they will most likely say that they are not sure what it is. But in reality, they just don't know how to explain it.

46. They don't know how to react.

While out with people, there are a lot of things that other people may say to an autistic child that he is not sure how to take. Innocent statements that may not offend others may offend him. Comments that may seem clear to some may be confusing to an autistic child. As result, he may not know how to respond to some things others may say to him.

47. Jokes may be taken too literally.

While I've never had a problem with taking things literally, I know other kids with autism have an issue with mishearing some jokes that others tell. This can lead to them feeling confused, amazed by a sarcastic comment, or offended.

48. Insults may be taken too personally.

Whenever someone says something to me that intends to hurt my feelings, I feel very down on myself and at the bottom of the world. I, along with several others like me, have very sensitive emotions that get hurt easily.

49. Autistic children have trouble sharing thoughts.

While out with friends, what drives the social event is everyone sharing their experiences. But that one person with autism just can't share her thoughts to the others. She is afraid of sounding either unusual or too different from the crowd.

50. Their words can come out wrong.

Again, I have this problem all the time. I say something one way and it comes out entirely different without me even knowing. As a result, others' feelings get hurt, or they may think I am being rude or snappy.

51. There's always the feeling of loneliness.

This is something I have had to deal with my whole life; seeing my friends going out with their closer friends, and never asking me to join. Seeing that from anyone's eyes can be enough to bring down their spirits. Keep encouraging your child to not give up, and they will find some true friends.

What is the Best Schooling Option?

52. Early intervention is an important step.

Start as young as possible visiting various doctors to find out your child's needs and getting an exact diagnosis. I was diagnosed with speech and language delay at two and began private therapy with a speech pathologist. This helped prepare me for finding the right preschool.

53. Diagnosing autism leads to better opportunities.

At age five I was diagnosed with Pervasive Developmental Disorder-Not Otherwise Specified, a type of autism. Because of this, I qualified for special services in my public school and was placed on an IEP (Individualized Education Program) from kindergarten through high school.

54. Individualized Education Programs help track learning

With the diagnosis of PDD-NOS, I was given the right to be placed on an IEP, which meant that I had a special education teacher assigned to my case, who met with my parents and worked with my other teachers to set and track goals for areas such as academics, behavior and communication.

55. School options for the elementary years.

My parents took advantage of the special services offered at my public elementary school. Your particular child though may fit at certain types of private schools such as Christian, Montessori, or special needs centers that work with autistic children.

56. If there is no verbal communication.

In this case the choices are a bit more limited. Based on the child's learning ability, it could be more appropriate for you to teach him. But there are other options, such as private schools and tutors who can communicate and teach in a way he can understand.

57. Consider how they interact with teachers.

Teachers are the main mentors of your child growing up. With autism, a child may love one teacher, but feel uncomfortable with another. For me, the top priority of my learning and school experience was being comfortable with the person teaching me. The best teacher could be a parent.

58. Is making friends always a priority?

There might be a time during your child's school years where social skills should become a lower priority than academics. For me in seventh grade, making friends was less important than working in a productive learning environment, so I began home-schooling.

59. Transitioning between schools can be difficult.

Because of the difficult transition between elementary and middle school, my parents decided to homeschool me when I moved to middle school. For two years, my schooling consisted of classes at my public school, lessons at home with my parents, and classes at a smaller homeschool center. There are many options to consider when finding the right fit for your child.

60. Any schooling option can be changed.

My school career switched from public school to homeschool, then back to public school in ninth grade, which was right for me. While autistic children like predictability and consistency, don't look at any schooling decision as one that must continue until graduation.

Transitions in School as they Age

61. Teachers can make a big impact.

I was blessed to attend school in a good public school district and am thankful for the many caring teachers, principals, counselors and others who had good knowledge of how to work with autistic children, and had love, care and concern for me. Great teachers combined with parent involvement helped me to learn and grow, both academically and socially.

62. The teachers are not always terrific.

There were also a few teachers along the way who did not fit my learning style. Work with the administrators to find the best teachers who fit your child's needs; being involved with parent teacher organizations and helping in class will help get to know teachers as well.

63. Every grade's harder than the last.

There's a reason why each grade is given a number; it shows the increasing difficulty, which is especially noticeable for autistic children. Get to know the teachers and stay involved with your child's homework so you can help your child advance from each grade to the next.

64. There's that unexpected amount of homework.

For autistic students, anything that is more than expected is very difficult. Because they like their life to be the same every day, homework duties are especially difficult. Work with the teacher to help your child know what to expect.

65. Every school has a big bully.

Autism can make your child a target of the school bully. Keeping in clear communication with your child, as well as his teachers and other parents will help you know what's going on, and help control the bullying.

66. They may fall under the influence.

Some autistic kids may not have the right judgment when offered drugs or alcohol. Is taking these pills bad? Is what this kid is saying about cigarettes being "not so bad" true? Be very specific when explaining substance abuse to your child.

67. New schools mean meeting new people.

Going to new schools, whether middle school, high school or college has been hard for me because of all the new unfamiliar students. I can take as long as six months to connect with friends, and even longer to know who my real friends are.

68. Switching schools is hard to do.

When I started going to college, everything became more difficult because I was in a new location with new people and a new learning style. It is challenging for others like me to make this big of an adjustment.

69. Being away from parents is difficult.

When your child goes to college, he or she might be away from you. They take longer than others to accept that they're apart from their parents, and need extra help to get over the negative feelings of extreme separation.

70. The subjects are beyond their interests.

All students are required to attend classes they consider boring, in which they have little or no interest. An autistic child would not be as accepting of this, because they are even more narrow and obsessive about the things about which they are truly interested.

71. They walk from class to class.

As I've said earlier, some like me can focus only on one single subject. College could clearly be a frustrating time slumping from class to class on a large campus, and the amount of work, all from different classes, can be overwhelming.

Major Life Events are Especially Challenging

72. Moving starts a whole new chapter.

In their old home, a child knew where everything was, but in a new home, he suddenly can't find anything and has to start all over with his daily activities and routines. Let him know beforehand where all of his personal items will be so he will feel more comfortable with the new house.

73. It's a boy! It's a girl!

I am the youngest in my family, so I never had to experience having a little sibling. For autistic children who have to adjust having a new baby brother or sister, take extra care to prepare him for what to expect, and give him an even mix of separation and one-on-one time with the other sibling.

74. "Daddy won't live with us anymore."

While divorce devastates everyone, it is especially hard for your autistic child because it upsets his orderly world. If divorce happens, try to maintain his routine as much as possible, and give him plenty of advance details about visiting schedules and any other changes at home. Help him stay in contact with the other parent with social networking, phone, and Skype, depending on his age.

75. "Daddy has a new wife now."

As if divorce wasn't bad enough for your child imagine if her mom or dad got remarried to someone else! Try to be accommodating when the child requests time with her biological parent. The adjustment will take time and patience. Keep your autistic child informed of plans and developments so she is not surprised.

76. The parent's new partner moves in.

When it comes to divorce, your child may have no choice but to live with the divorced parent's new partner. This is a major challenge for an autistic child. To make it easier, work with both your partner and child to get to know each other better and explain how the new arrangement will work.

77. The new partner brings in siblings.

There is a chance the new partner may bring in sons and daughters of her own, requiring your autistic child to adjust to stepsiblings at home. Spend extra time helping the stepsiblings learn about autism and your child's specific challenges. Look for things they have in common, and help them get to know each other.

78. The nanny is here. Now what?

If you are planning to hire a nanny, introduce your child to her several times beforehand, and let her join you for dinner several times. Make sure the nanny familiarizes herself with autism and your child's needs before starting the job. Schedules and routines will be helpful for everyone involved.

79. The older sibling must move on.

I had to let my sister go when she left home to attend college. The instant I realized she was gone, it was difficult for me to accept. But in time, I got used to it. It helped to know when I would see her again, whether she was coming home, or we were going to visit her. We also kept in touch through Facebook.

80. Relatives who stay for much longer.

Every now and then, you may have a relative who stays at your house for an extended time. This type of change upsets your child's daily routine and involves unfamiliar people, so make an effort to help your child get to know the relatives by filling him in about them before they arrive. Let the relatives know how to relate to your child as well. If they are sleeping in his room, give your child a space where he can have his own things, have time alone, and create a new, temporary routine.

Forgiving and Forgetting About the Past

81. They hold on to their grudges.

Looking back ten years ago, I am still annoyed at someone for either hurting my feelings or simply being an annoying pest. For other kids with this problem, they should be reminded about the more friendly people they know today.

82. Guilt gets the better of them.

Realizing my wrongs brings down my spirits tremendously throughout the day. If your autistic child has this issue, clearly explain that what they did wasn't so bad compared to what other kids their age often do in the same situation.

83. Their memories are sharp and vivid.

With some autistic people, such as me, their memories are so precise that they remember the little details in a situation that others do not. Keep this in mind while encouraging your child to put those painful memories behind him.

84. A situation can make them opinionated.

Your child may feel strongly about a certain viewpoint, which could originate from a past experience he had. This experience could change the way he sees everything today, so help your child focus on the true current issues.

85. They often keep track of people.

If your child has a problem with tolerating someone they consider intolerable, help him organize a T-chart for that person--one side for the person's good qualities, the other for bad qualities. This helps give your child a more realistic viewpoint.

86. It is hard to forget negativity.

Having a narrative look on life, I find it difficult to let the past go because it made me who I am today. Work with your child to see that it is okay to remember the past, but not overly dwell on it.

87. They'll look back and feel bad.

Remember that one time your child broke the cookie jar fifteen years ago and you scolded him? Well, because of his vivid memory, he is still mentally scarred by the painful memory. It is important to be understanding if he feels bad about past experiences.

88. Feelings are too sensitive to forget.

Whenever I get an emotion, whether it is laughter or sadness or anger, it is more extreme than everyone else's. Your child will need you to help him talk through these emotions and keep them in perspective. Validate his feelings, but show him other viewpoints as well, keeping in mind his vivid memory.

89. They take things much too personally.

Someone may insult your child, either intentionally or unintentionally, and he will take it much harder than others would, keeping him from socializing with anyone. He really needs to hear your encouragement to stay away from negative thoughts.

90. Overreacting often results in negative thoughts.

Reflecting upon all the bad things I've done in the past has made me vulnerable to feelings of self-hate and worthlessness. Solutions may require anything from counseling, positive encouragement, or, when younger, simply distracting him with an activity to take his mind off of things.

Daily Dealing with your Autistic Child

91. How they'll interact with your friends.

Parents of autistic children are often concerned about how their child will present himself to your friends, knowing that he may say something inappropriate. Try to anticipate each situation and remind your child specifically how to interact with guests each time.

92. You'll hear new stories every day.

Many days, your child may come home from school feeling overwhelmed by the busy, difficult environment. Be patient with starting after-school activities and have an open ear to hear what your child might want to tell you about his day.

93. They don't feel sharing is caring.

I have never liked to share my personal interests or thoughts, because I felt they were too different from everyone else. For your child, help him to bring out those thoughts once in a while rather than all at once.

94. Relationships are not always a priority.

Many autistic people would rather spend time inside their minds instead of with others. It is your duty as a parent to bring your child out of his comfort zone and aid him in engaged conversations with people he knows.

95. They are sensitive to almost everything.

Whether it is touch, sound, sight, taste, or smell, a child with autism is sensitive to anything extreme. This is when it's always good to have something such as a stress toy or hug machine to help him calm down.

96. Get their siblings on their side.

Your nonautistic sons and daughters can help your autistic child overcome daily pressures. Keep them just as educated about the autistic child as you are, and perhaps even let them read this book. This will benefit them when they get older.

97. Phone a therapist- they can help!

I've talked with a therapist who specialized in working with teenagers with autism, who showed understanding and helped by talking me through my struggles and concerns. Ask your child's school counselors for recommendations if you think your child needs an outside counselor.

98. Give them time on their own.

Being out with so many people for too much time creates a very overwhelming atmosphere for your child. So, if at any time, he says he needs some time by himself, give it to him; because it does help him.

99. Give them patience, let them think.

If something comes up suddenly for me, I don't know how to take it. If I am just given about fifteen minutes to mull it over and process the thought, I can be more reasonable about accepting the change.

100. Put love as your top priority.

While growing up, my parents always made sure I knew they loved me. This helped significantly in bringing my spirits up. Every day, tell your child you love him, but not too much, or he will feel uncomfortable with you.

More about the Author

Trevor Pacelli grew up in Sammamish, Washington. As a child, he published drawings in two children's magazines, and at age 15 he illustrated a children's autism awareness book, **The Kindergarten Adventures of Amazing Grace**, authored by his older sister, Briana Pacelli.

Trevor studies film and media at Arizona State University and blogs about current films at **TrevorPacelli.com**.

See the entire Six-Word Lesson Series at **6wordlessons.com**

Discover more books and resources about autism at **GrowingUpAutistic.com**

More books on Autism

Available on GrowingUpAutistic.com in paperback and e-book

Six-Word Lessons on Growing Up Autistic

by Trevor Pacelli

50 Things You Should Know About Me

by Trevor Pacelli

The Kindergarten Adventures of Amazing Grace

by Briana Pacelli

Six-Word Lessons for Autism Friendly Workplaces

by Patty Pacelli

Six-Word Lessons on Females with Asperger's Syndrome

by Tracey Cohen

Connect with Growing Up Autistic

Facebook.com/GrowingUpAutistic

Twitter @GrowingUpAutism

Growing Up Autistic - 50 Things You Should Know about Me

Trevor Pacelli

GrowingUpAutistic.com

Introduction

Trevor Pacelli was diagnosed with autism at age five, and was the first in his extended family to have autism. Growing up autistic impacted his family in many ways. As an autistic adult, he wants parents and younger children to learn about autism first-hand, so they use his experiences to know what to expect and how to cope with the challenges. Autism is a broad spectrum, and every person on the spectrum is different, but there are also similarities. Trevor has answered these 50 questions with the transparent honesty typical of autistic individuals, and it is his hope that children, parents, relatives and caregivers can learn from his insight.

1. Who were the parental figures who primarily raised you in your home?

My mom, Patty Pacelli, and my Dad, Lonnie Pacelli

2. How old were you when you were diagnosed with autism?

I think I was five and a half years old.

3. How old were you when you learned that you were autistic?

I don't remember a specific age when I found out I was autistic.

4. Did you understand what autism was?

When I first heard the word, I didn't know exactly what it was. It was one of those things where I just gradually learned more about it as I got older.

5. What types of therapy did you receive, and how did it help your autism?

I had private speech and language therapy starting at 2, then worked with speech language pathologists, school psychologists and special education teachers from elementary school through high school. The therapy and other programs helped me to learn more about the structure of a conversation and how I should interact with others.

6. What were your eating habits like as a child?

I really liked to eat at the same times every day, and our family was on a pretty consistent eating schedule.

7. Were you a picky eater?

I was very, very picky as a child. In restaurants, I would only order French fries and grilled cheese sandwiches, and I didn't even try my first cheeseburger until I was nine.

8. How have your eating habits changed?

Now, I will eat basically anything. I still pick out foods in dishes such as onions or tomatoes, but am brave in trying new foods.

9. How did you handle changes in routine when you were a child?

I was someone who would always whine, cry and fall to the ground whenever I was told there was a change in routine.

10. How do you handle changes in routine now?

I still get upset and mildly agitated, but I try my best to change my mindset.

11. Did you like physical contact, such as hugs when you were a child?

Yes.

12. Do you like physical contact now?

Yes, just the same.

13. How did you handle vacations as a child?

I would always find a reason to complain, which ended in me whining and crying on the ground because I didn't like the sudden change in routine.

14. How do you handle vacations now?

I handle them perfectly fine like any person would.

15. How did you handle things you disliked (i.e., loud noises) as a child?

Just like I handled vacations, I would wine and cry a lot.

16. How do you handle things you dislike now?

I handle it more maturely and keep it to myself, in fact so much to myself, that I never open it up to others.

17. How did you get along with your sibling(s) as a child?

I did not get along with my sister much at all. We had our "best-friend" moments, but most of our time together was a lot of bickering.

18. How is your relationship with your sibling(s) today?

My sister and I are much closer now that we used to be. We fight much less often, and enjoy spending time together.

19. Were there things that you obsessed about when you were a child? If so, what were they?

Absolutely. I've obsessed over Blue's Clues, Pokémon, *and* SpongeBob.

20. Do you still obsess about things now?

I definitely obsess over things now.

21. Are they different things?

Some I've sort of held on to, but I always move on to and from different things. One has been the Lion King Musical.

22. Did you have friends when you were a child?

I had other kids that I would play with, but never someone I knew personally.

23. Do you have friends now?

I have people that I know on a good, personal level, but only a small handful.

24. As a child, what did you want to be when you grew up?

When I was little, I wanted to be a giraffe, but gradually started wanting to be a movie director.

25. What do you want to be/are you now?

Now, I want to be a filmmaker in Hollywood, possibly a director.

26. What was your favorite thing about school as a child?

The art projects, because I got to put my imagination on paper, and all the other kids commented on how good I was at it.

27. What was your least favorite thing about school as a child?

Any "special days" we had where we did something out of the routine, such as classroom parties or all-grade lunches.

28. How do you feel your teachers treated you as a child?

I felt my elementary school teachers understood me and my needs, but not even in the least when I got to high school.

29. What was your best subject in school?

Art

30. What was your worst subject in school?

Science

31. What advice would you give teachers of autistic students?

Know precisely what their special needs are, because it is highly crucial to their learning and developmental process of growing and maturing.

32. What were your favorite books as a child?

I used to love reading The Bailey School Kids books, as well as the Dr. Seuss books.

33. What are your favorite books now?

I haven't read a book for pleasure in a long time, but I love all the Harry Potter books.

34. What were your favorite movies as a child?

I liked Disney movies such as The Lion King, Hercules, *and* Aladdin.

35. What are your favorite movies now?

I like more mature, artsy films such as American Beauty, Titanic, *and* Life of Pi. *But I also like more fun films like* Back to the Future *and* Star Wars.

36. Are there any public figures (celebrities, athletes, etc.) you look up to?

Steven Spielberg

37. Do you ever feel like you've positively impacted or inspired someone else?

I know that I have, but I don't truly feel it.

38. Do you drive a car? How old were you when you got your driver's license?

Yes, I drive and got my license at 16.

39. Do you use public transportation?

I do, but I don't often like using things like the bus.

40. Have you ever had a paying job?

I have worked in the kitchen for a summer camp, and did maintenance and security for my church.

41. How did your autism affect job-hunting, interviewing and working, and what did you *learn from it?*

In the application and interview processes, I would often misread what someone was asking me, and give them an answer that wasn't what they were looking for. Through having a job, I learned more about how to commit myself to something and maintain positivity.

42. Have you wanted a boyfriend or girlfriend?

Yes

43. Have you ever had a boyfriend or girlfriend?

No.

44. Do you want to be a father/mother someday?

Maybe, I could just be underestimating the responsibility though.

45. Are you able to live independently and take care of yourself now? If not, what are you not able to do for yourself?

I am able to take care of myself very manageably and be independent.

46. What do you feel is your greatest strength now?

The ability to plan out images in my head before putting it on paper.

47. What do you feel is your greatest weakness now?

Any kind of sport such as basketball or volleyball.

48. Is there anything you feel you can't do because of your autism?

Lots: make friends, sit still, and focus for longer than five minutes, etcetera.

49. What advice would you give parents of an autistic child?

Don't do anything to them if you know it will upset them, accommodate as much as you can.

50. What advice would you give an autistic child?

The world's not always going to play by your rules, you're in their world too. Learn to watch yourself so that you act "socially presentable" enough to not draw too much negative attention to yourself.

27 Tips to Conquer the Seven Deadly Sins of Leadership

Lonnie Pacelli

LonniePacelli.com

Summary

Pride. Envy. Gluttony. Lust. Anger. Greed. Sloth. You either recognize these as the seven deadly sins or as themes for prime-time television. Nonetheless, you were probably taught as a child that these are bad and you shouldn't do them. For purposes of this Action Guide, do as you were taught and think bad when you commit these similar sins in the workplace.

As leaders, we are continually being introduced to new techniques and theories. Hammer & Champy's Business Process Re-engineering Model, McKinsey's 7-S Framework, and Kenichi Ohmae's 3C's Strategic Triangle are all examples of strategic models designed to help leaders think about their business in different and innovative ways. What sits on top of all of the models and frameworks, though, are a series of foundational attributes that every leader should possess if he or she is going to have demonstrated, sustained success as a leader.

In my career as a leader, I've been fortunate enough to experience a broad array of leadership situations where sometimes I enjoyed fantastic success, and at other times experienced dismal failure. In looking back at my failures, many of them had nothing to do with a theory, framework, or technology that was utilized. The failures had to do with cracks in my own foundational attributes which left me vulnerable as a leader. I've boiled these down to seven key sins which this seminar will focus on to help you become a more effective leader.

Topic #1 – The Sin of Arrogance

Jack just returned from his manager's staff meeting muttering to himself. Ron, a colleague from another department, couldn't help but ask Jack what was wrong. "They just don't get it!" he sputtered. "I must work with the biggest bunch of fools in the company!" Ron was intrigued, "How so?" he asked. "Here's one for starters," Jack began. "We were going through department budgets, and I couldn't believe the excuses I was hearing about why my peers were over budget. It was one lame excuse after another and nothing but whining and complaining. What a bunch of morons!" Ron asked, "Were you over budget?" "Well, yes," Jack explained. "But I was the only one with a reasonable explanation of why I was over budget. Everyone else just whined and complained. What a bunch of inept lug nuts!" Ron politely excused himself, "Hang in there, Jack," he said while walking away thankful that he wasn't one of Jack's peers.

Regardless of whether you work with peers, lead a team, or work for another leader, carrying an air of superiority towards others is flat out uninspiring. As a leader, your team is expecting you to do the right thing regardless of where the idea comes from. Many leaders confuse being a good leader with having all the answers to problems. The truth is that the best leaders may not always **have** the right answer, but they will usually know where to **find** the right answer. The answer can come from a colleague, customer, supplier, employee, or manager. The important thing is to look above, around, and below to uncover the best solution to problems and to use the strength of those around you to make a good solution even better. Remember, it's truly about getting things done as effectively as possible, not who came up with the idea.

Topic #1 - Is this me?

Review each question and ask yourself if the question sounds like something you have done or would do.

I like to talk about my accomplishments

I think it's important to use success to establish credibility with peers

I like to compete with my colleagues when talking about successes

I feel there isn't much I can learn from my colleagues

I like to debate those that have viewpoints which differ from my own

I am very confident I can handle any problem thrown at me without the help of others

I believe openly discussing failures with colleagues is wrong

I see my failures as a result of things others have done wrong, not what I have done wrong

I seldom praise my peers on their accomplishments

Topic #2 – The Sin of Indecisiveness

On Monday you sit down with your manager to discuss a problem which requires a decision. You leave the meeting thinking a decision has been made and proceed forward with the plan to implement the decision. On Wednesday, you learn from a colleague that the manager has re-thought his decision and wants to pursue a different course of action. On Thursday you meet with your manager to discuss the about-face, and the manager agrees that the original course of action is the right course to take. On the following Monday the manager calls a staff meeting to discuss the issue again. Sound familiar?

Whether you're a CEO, small business owner, or an apprentice, decision making is something you do each and every day. Whether the decision is about buying a company, hiring an employee, or choosing a lunch restaurant, the decision making components are essentially the same. At its core, most every decision is comprised of the following components:

- A need that must be fulfilled

- A deadline the need must be fulfilled by

- The impact of **not** fulfilling the need

- Choices for fulfilling the need and associated consequences of each choice

- Credible Information that supports each choice

The best decision makers I have seen intuitively understand these five components and make decisions based upon simultaneously meeting each of these components. When any one of these components isn't clearly understood and agreed upon by the decision maker and associated stakeholders, faulty decision making is likely to occur. The faulty decision making results in either a poor decision or a decision that doesn't get made. Either way, precious time and resources are lost.

Being a good decision maker means that you not only adhere to the above components, but that you involve stakeholders (those that will be affected by the decision) and subject matter experts (those who can contribute information to each choice and consequence) in the decision making process. Including both of these groups in the decision making process not only ensures a more holistic decision but also creates the buy-in necessary to effectively implement the decision.

Regardless of your level or number of people you lead, you will have decisions to make that will affect others. Keeping these basic decision making principles in mind will help you slay the indecisiveness beast.

Topic #2 - Is this me?

Review each question and ask yourself if the question sounds like something you have done or would do.

I tend to "un-decide" things that have already been decided upon

I usually ask for additional information on an issue more than once before attempting to make a decision

I strive for perfection and am reluctant to make a decision unless my view of perfection can be achieved

I am typically the last one to agree upon a decision when others are involved in decision making

I don't care if others get frustrated with me because I don't make decisions as quickly as they would like

I am uncomfortable with others making a decision on something that may impact me

I typically play "Monday Morning Quarterback" with decisions I've already made

I mull decisions over regardless of how big or small they are

Topic #3 – The Sin of Disorganization

Fred's team nicknamed him "Taz." Recall back to your younger days watching Bugs Bunny cartoons. One of the characters was the Tasmanian Devil. Rather than move in a straight line, he would spin like a tornado and weave a destructive path wherever he went. When he finally stopped, he would pant wildly with his tongue hanging out while sputtering gibberish at whoever was nearby. Fred's mannerisms closely mirrored those of the Tasmanian Devil. He would rush into meetings ten minutes late, appear to be running in ten different directions at once, and regularly derail the team with his latest issue of the day. Fred saw his disorganization as part of his character and accepted it as a fact of life. Fred's team saw it as a disruption and a key barrier to the team being more effective.

Many leaders that are plagued with the Sin of Disorganization either don't view themselves as disorganized or say "that's just how I'm made." When it is just yourself that you need to be concerned with, then you can probably accept your own weakness and go on with life. The problem arises, though, when others are impacted. As leaders, you are expected to be navigating the ship and leading the team from source to destination. Imagine yourself as a skipper of a boat. You are expected to know where you want to go, how you're going to get there, when you're going to arrive, and what you're going to do if the unexpected happens. If you're running around the ship constantly changing direction, reacting frantically to rough waters, and arriving three days later than expected, you're going to frustrate your ship-mates and probably get thrown overboard.

The message here is simple; when you're disorganized and people are depending on you to lead, your disorganization will be amplified throughout your team and will create stress among your employees. Don't settle for being disorganized, your team is depending on you to conquer the sin and improve the effectiveness of not just yourself but the team as a whole.

Topic #3 – Is this me?

Review each question and ask yourself if the question sounds like something you have done or would do.

I'm frequently late for meetings

My workspace looks like a place where a tornado just touched down

I tend to lose things

I keep saying "I need to get organized"

I would read books on getting organized but I just don't have the time

I always feel as if I am rushing around

I typically get things done last-minute

I create fire drills for myself and others

I tend to stay up late at night getting things done to meet a deadline

My to-do list doesn't really reflect what I am working on right now

Topic #4 – The Sin of Stubbornness

I know of a young manager (let's call him "Author") who took on a fast-paced, high-risk three month project. At the end of the first month the project was almost an entire month behind schedule because of software installation problems. Author forged ahead despite the team's warning flares. At the end of the second month the project was almost two months behind schedule due to the installation problem in month one plus some development problems in month two. The team and the client desperately tried to tell Author they were in deep yogurt but still Author forged ahead. Author never got to see what happened in month three because Author's management removed him from the project due to his own stubbornness. Painful lesson indeed; I feel really bad for Author.

Decisiveness and determination are outstanding characteristics for any leader to have. Leaders who courageously forge ahead, aren't afraid to explore new territories, and are decisive when it comes to choosing alternatives are leaders who teams will align with. Where problems arise, though, is when decisiveness and determination give way to stubbornness. Once stubbornness sets in, the leader can be viewed as not being a team player and will quickly alienate his team. It's only a matter of time before the leader will be voted off the island.

To clearly highlight my point, I'm going to give you a simple equation, as follows:

Decisiveness + Determination – Listening = Stubbornness

Leaders who drive solutions and aren't afraid to make decisions, but are unwilling to listen to team members or colleagues, are afflicted with the Sin of Stubbornness. When leaders take an attitude of "I know best" and refuse to listen to other viewpoints, they are going to quickly get out of step with their team and be branded as stubborn. This doesn't mean you have to blindly accept and implement any viewpoint thrown your way; but it means you have to be open to listening and rational about accepting an alternative viewpoint.

The moral of this story is clear: By all means be determined and decisive in your execution. Just remember to listen to others' viewpoints and implement those viewpoints that make sense. As long as a job gets done successfully, who cares where the ideas came from?

Topic #4 - Is this me?

Review each question and ask yourself if the question sounds like something you have done or would do.

I have a hard time accepting viewpoints that are counter to my own

I will continue to do something despite warnings from others that I should stop

I hate getting constructive feedback on my performance

I allowed a failed project that was under my leadership go on longer than it should have

My team or colleagues tend to gang up on me during discussions

I have a hard time admitting something was my fault

I've heard feedback that I'm stubborn, but I just see myself as determined

I apply the phrase "I'm not going down without a fight" to most aspects of my life

Even if I think another viewpoint might be as good as my own, I'll still choose my viewpoint over another's

I believe the best way to learn is to make your own mistakes

Topic #5 – The Sin of Negativism

Kelly was dreading her meeting with her manager, Bill. Bill could be the poster child for negativity. It didn't matter how good an idea someone had, Bill would always bring up some negative aspect of the idea and make the person feel worthless. In the past, Bill was asked about his negativity. "I'm a critical thinker," Bill said. "If I flush out the things that could go wrong with an idea there will be better likelihood of success."

Kelly started into the meeting and presented her idea to Bill. Bill shifted into "critical thinking mode" and immediately started telling Kelly what could go wrong with her idea. Kelly listened politely, realizing that she wasn't going to get anywhere with Bill. She left the meeting, went back to her desk, and started updating her resume.

OK, so you most likely know what being negative looks like; it's the "glass is half empty" person who manages to find the bad in just about any topic or any person. What may not be obvious, though, is how a negative leader impacts his or her team. As a leader, you hold a lot of power over those you lead. With a single phrase you can either brighten someone's day or ruin it. A sideways glance can cause a team member to worry about his or her job. Similarly, having a negative attitude puts a black cloud over the team and creates an environment of negativity. If the leader is negative, the team will carry the attributes of the leader and will be negative which will ultimately lead to lost effectiveness.

Now, I'm not advocating that you as leader become a nauseating shiny happy person who hands out candy to your team and holds morning cheerleading sessions. What I am saying is you have to balance being positive with being pragmatic. If you strip away the pragmatic side of the equation, you become someone who will cheerfully walk into a lion's den. If you are pragmatic without being positive, you run the risk of being negative. In either event, the team will not want to follow you.

As my comic book hero Spiderman says, "With great power comes great responsibility." Accept the responsibility given to you as a leader and be pragmatically positive in your leadership. Your team will follow you and you'll be more effective in getting things done.

Topic #5 - Is this me?

Review each question and ask yourself if the question sounds like something you have done or would do.

I tend to look at what is wrong with a solution versus what is right

I enjoy playing the role of "devil's advocate"

I tend to see the negative characteristics in people

I at times complain to colleagues about my job or my management

I generally avoid giving praise to others

I think team-building activities are a waste of time

I am typically one of the first to say "I told you so" when something goes wrong

Topic #6 – The Sin of Cowardice

I once worked with a client manager who had difficulty with being held accountable for his actions. If there was a problem on the project, the client spent time in the meeting playing "cover-your-butt" and blaming others for any of the project problems. Ultimately the client manager was replaced primarily because he was unwilling to accept responsibility for problems on the project. Both the project team and the manager's management had lost faith in his ability to deliver results.

Being a leader means you're expected to cover new ground, take some risks, execute well, and be held accountable for your performance. Many of today's leaders have difficulty with the "being held accountable" requirement of leadership and will either avoid taking on the hard stuff or look to shift blame when things go south. This becomes even more difficult for some leaders when they are held accountable not only for their own actions, but for those of their team. When the Enron scandal happened in 2002, their auditor, Arthur Andersen & Co., was implicated and its CEO, Joseph Berardino, was required to answer questions in a very public forum about what happened at Enron. Regardless of how much or how little he was involved, the buck stopped with him and he was held accountable for the actions of the Firm.

Those leaders who avoid accountability either through taking the easy road or shifting blame are afflicted in a big way with the Sin of Cowardice. When things get difficult, their modus operandi is to protect their own backside and allow someone else to take the fall. Would you fly on a plane where you knew the pilot would be the first one to bail out if turbulence hit? Doubtful. Similarly, it is incredibly difficult to follow a leader who bails on his or her team at the first sign of trouble.

The point here is that leaders need to be willing to be held accountable for anything that happens under their watch and have to take the bullet for the team with their management regardless of who on the team messed up. Any leader who doesn't is showing his or her cowardice stripes and isn't going to get a team to willingly follow him or her.

Topic #6 - Is this me?

Review each question and ask yourself if the question sounds like something you have done or would do.

I tend to look at what others have done wrong when determining root causes on problems

I have a hard time explicitly admitting in front of my management that I have screwed up

I can at times shift blame to others

I finger-point in meetings

I don't take on hard projects

I strongly avoid getting out of my comfort zone

I am relieved when someone else is getting blamed for something

I don't like trying new things

Topic #7 – The Sin of Untrustworthiness

"Don't tell anyone, but…."

How many times have you heard someone say that to you right before they were going to give you some juicy piece if information? Interestingly enough, it's as if by saying "don't tell anyone, but…" in front of a statement you have now given yourself a get-out-of-jail-free card to distribute the information because you have the impression that the recipient of your message is actually going to heed your warning. But, sure as the day you're born your recipient will turn around and tell someone else "don't tell anyone, but…" then divulge the scrumptious morsel. This seems to continue until the tantalizing tidbit is no more tantalizing then it starts all over again with another juicy bit. Welcome to the grapevine.

I am the first to admit that I have participated in grapevine fodder. I have also done things in my younger years that have called my trustworthiness into question. I have regretted those actions because they have caused my team, peers, and management to question my leadership capabilities. I learned some very important lessons on how leaders have to be super careful about doing anything that calls their trustworthiness or integrity into question. If others don't believe you then you won't get others to follow you.

Leaders, hear this: **Do what you say and say what you do.** Words that don't mirror actions and actions that don't support words are the key drivers for questioning your trustworthiness. If you commit to saying or not saying, doing or not doing something **then live up to it**. Once your trustworthiness is questioned it takes a long time for that question to go away.

Do what you say and say what you do. It's the cleanest path to avoiding the Sin of Untrustworthiness.

Topic #7 - Is this me?

Review each question and ask yourself if the question sounds like something you have done or would do.

I at times don't deliver on commitments I make to others

I have been told I am unreliable

I feel that my manager micro-manages me

I dislike being held accountable for commitments

I at times will just not show up for an appointment

I am typically late for meetings

I will make commitments that I know I can't deliver upon just to appease someone

My actions don't always back up my words

I at times repeat something to a colleague that someone else told me "not to tell anyone"

Putting it into action

So you've gone through each topic and assessed yourself against some key questions. What next?

The next step is to develop a Personal Action Plan based on the results of your self-assessment. First, decide which 1-3 focus topics to address. Then decide on up to three tangible actions for each focus item to help you create new habits. As input to the tangible actions, use the ideas matrix in this section to help jump-start some creative ways to address your focus topics.

Here are some things to consider as you're developing your Personal Action Plan:

Make sure your actions are clear, concise, tangible, and easy to understand.

Keep your focus topics to no more than three areas. Trying to work with too many focus topics will dilute your efforts and reduce your likelihood of success.

Keep your actions to no more than three per focus topic. As with focus topics, the more actions you try to take on, the less likely you'll do any of them well (if at all). Get very precise on a few actions and nail them.

Be realistic. Don't get overly aggressive with your action items and set yourself up for failure. Pick a few precise, high-impact reasonable actions and execute.

Your action plan should be personal, relevant, and applicable to you and your position. No one can or should develop an action plan for you. The best action plans are developed by the owner and utilize at least one coach (a trusted colleague, team member, or family member) who can observe you "in action" and help you build new habits.

As food for thought, use the following list of ideas to help you jump-start your action plan. You may use some or none of the below ideas, just make sure your actions are personal, relevant and applicable to you.

Arrogance

Choose three failures and honestly document what you personally could have done to avoid the failure

Become an advocate within your organization for someone else's idea

Interview three colleagues on a recent success they achieved

Prepare a lessons learned presentation on a recent failure and present it to colleagues or your team

Choose a recent problem you've had and document who could have helped you solve the problem

Praise calculated risk-taking with your team, even if it resulted in failure

Indecisiveness

Physically write out the five components for each major decision: the need, date needed, impact of not making a decision, choices and consequences, and information needed

Keep a log of outstanding decisions you need to make and their associated needed-by date and commit to making the decisions by the needed-by date

Implement a standing decision-making meeting with your team where you review outstanding decisions and commit to making decisions as a team

Disorganization

Spend 15 minutes each morning planning out your day

Practice only handling pieces of information once

Keep a prioritized to-do list sequenced by need date.

Keep a list of "Big Ideas" (to-do's that are important but aren't time-sensitive)

Schedule to-do's into your calendar, including a bit of time for your "Big Ideas"

Schedule personal time (exercise, dinner, etc.) into your calendar

Stubbornness

Run major ideas or problems by a trusted colleague and physically write down their feedback

Actively ask for feedback from your team on ideas and write down their feedback

Practice incorporating someone's feedback into your idea and demonstrate back to the team how the feedback was incorporated

Negativism

When offering feedback, provide at least one positive comment for every negative comment

Phrase negative feedback in terms of "here's a suggestion to make it better"

Before offering negative feedback, briefly ask yourself "Is this feedback important enough to give?"

Cowardice

When faced with a problem, physically write down the answer to the following question: "What could I do to avoid this from occurring or avoid making it worse?"

Take on one project that you know will push you out of your comfort zone

Develop a lessons-learned list from a project outlining what things went wrong on the project and what you specifically could have done to avoid the problem. Review the list with your manager and your team

Untrustworthiness

Practice being five minutes early for every meeting you attend

Whenever someone says "don't tell anyone, but…" commit you will not pass it forward to anyone else; also commit that you will never initiate a "don't tell anyone, but…"

Keep a list of commitments you make, who you made it to, and the date you committed. Meet your commitments 100% of the time.

Some final thoughts

Change is hard. Change takes time. Change can be frustrating. But change for the better is always worth it.

Be patient with yourself.

Don't take on too much at once; focus on just one or two things and do them well.

Use a trusted friend or advisor to help you in your change journey.

You have to really want to change for it to happen. If you don't want it don't bother doing it.

Don't give up. You won't regret it.

About the Author

Lonnie Pacelli is an internationally recognized project management and leadership development expert with over 30 years' experience working with Fortune 100 organizations. His no-nonsense style helps get to the root of problems quickly and delivers sustainable results.

Find out more about Lonnie at LonniePacelli.com

17 Tips to Help You Find True Work/Life Balance

Lonnie Pacelli

LonniePacelli.com

Copyright 2013 by Lonnie Pacelli. All Rights Reserved.

Summary

So let's talk about over-used terms for a minute.

If you've been in the business world since the mid 1990s you've likely heard your management espouse the desire for employees to achieve greater work/life balance. Many U.S. companies have adopted programs to help employees strike a better life balance by providing health club benefits, entertainment discount programs, and additional time off for events such as the birth of a child. Despite all this, Americans are of the most overworked and flat-out busy people on earth, recently surpassing the Japanese and long surpassing the Europeans. With all this discussion of work/life balance, how can we in the U.S. also be of the most overworked people in the world? The answer is pretty simple; many of us **talk** work/life balance, but don't **live** work/life balance primarily because we don't know how to do it.

First let's get clear on the primary purpose of achieving work/life balance. It's about **minimizing stress** in your life. Much of the stress in a typical person's life is derived from work. You can say you've got work/life balance, but in addition to working full-time, you might participate in many activities with the kids, volunteer at the local homeless shelter, and exercise five days a week. If you're feeling stressed and tired you haven't achieved the primary intent of work/life balance, which is to reduce stress. **All you have done is balanced the degree of stress you have in your work life with the stress you have in your non-work life. But at least the stress is balanced ☺.**

Before we get too deep in this seminar, I want to get a couple of points on the table:

Work/life balance doesn't mean you never have to burn the midnight oil to get a project done. There will be times you will need to work hard to meet a deadline. What work/life balance does mean, though, is that burning the midnight oil will only be an exception, not a regular event.

Achieving work/life balance doesn't give you a get-out-of-jail-free card to not work hard or only work a few hours a week. We were meant to work and to provide for ourselves. It just means that work is done in moderation and not to an extreme.

Realizing the quest for work/life balance means doing some serious soul searching. The first focus topic in this action guide is designed to get you thinking about what is truly important to you. If you acknowledge you are a workaholic and don't want to change, then this action guide will probably be meaningless to you. If you do want to change, though, you'll get a few helpful nuggets from what you're about to read.

Topic #1 – Consciously (and honestly) decide what is really important

It was 9 p.m. and Phil was still at work. This was normal for Phil, who routinely worked 70 hours per week. Whenever he wasn't at work, he would either be on email or would be talking on the phone with a client, supplier, or colleague. His wife, Rose, was at the end of her rope. Phil's obsession with work and absence at home were taking a toll on her and their two children, both in elementary school. Rose decided to confront Phil about his work habits over the weekend.

On Sunday afternoon, Rose suggested to Phil they go to their local coffee shop to talk. After they grabbed a latte, Rose opened up to Phil, "I know that you want to provide a good life for us," Rose started, "but you're an absent father and husband and I need you to be more focused on our family and less focused on work." Phil listened intently and agreed with Rose that he had been prioritizing work over family. "I appreciate you telling me this, Rose," Phil said, "You and the kids are the most important thing to me. I'll work on this and will get better balanced." Rose was relieved that Phil was so receptive but was secretly skeptical that Phil would be able to put some long term change in place.

For a few days Phil made dramatic changes. He was home by 6 p.m. every night and was not nearly as preoccupied with email and his cell-phone while at home. Slowly, though, Phil drifted back to his old habits. "There are just too many important things going on at work that needs to be done yesterday," Phil would explain to Rose.

This cycle continued for months. Rose would confront Phil about his work habits, Phil would make a short-term improvement, and then some hot project would come up which caused Phil to go back to 70 hour work weeks. Rose ultimately gave up, knowing that even though Phil told her that she and the kids were most important, it was really his job that was most important in his life.

Maybe this sounds familiar; maybe it's a friend, relative, significant other, spouse, or you. Saying that work/life balance is important is one thing; truly meaning it is a different game altogether. You may **want** to believe you place other things above work, but wanting to believe it simply doesn't mean it's so. Now, it's not my job to sit in judgment of your priorities. If you want to prioritize your work and career above all else then go for it. The question you have to ask yourself, though, is whether that is what you really want.

Make a conscious, realistic declaration on where your priorities lie, then examine your behaviors or ask a friend, relative, significant other, or spouse. Taking the first step towards the quest for work/life balance means eliminating the gap between what you **desire** and what you **do**.

Topic #1 - Is this me?

Review each question and ask yourself if the question sounds like something you have done or would do.

I routinely work over 60 hours per week

I at times miss important social or family events because of my job

I find it very difficult to find the time to meet up with friends

My actions don't match my words when it comes to work/life balance

My spouse or significant other has confronted me about my work/life priorities

Topic #2 – Make your calendar a life thing, not just a work thing

Early on in my career I was very disciplined with my work calendar. I kept a good meeting schedule, blocked off time to do housekeeping things like email, and took good care to work my schedule. I was feeling very happy with myself that was so disciplined with my schedule at work and could be so productive.

In all of my pride and discipline I failed to address a major blind spot in my calendar; scheduling non-work activities. Left to my own devices, I would stay at work every waking hour of the day. There always seemed to be something important that I had to get done which would pre-empt family activities. I would come home at night to a table with a lone place setting and the kids all ready for bed. Despite all of my great scheduling habits at work, I was a big zero when it came to scheduling and keeping non-work commitments.

So it's confession time, colleagues. This is something I will struggle with until the day I die. I can get so preoccupied with my work that I will forget about doing things with my family. I can sit in church; get an idea for a new book, article, or action guide, and start jotting it down on my PDA right in the middle of the Pastor's sermon. I need constant reminders that work doesn't automatically trump other activities and need to actually schedule important non-work activities into my calendar.

Now, I don't want to give you the impression that I have my life scheduled out to the minute and curl up into a fetal position if I deviate from my calendar. What I have learned to do, though, is to integrate important personal activities into my calendar. Some examples of things I schedule include:

Exercise – I have 5 times a week exercise placeholders in my calendar. I can move the times around to accommodate other appointments, but don't delete the placeholders.

Dinner – We have an agreed-upon family dinner time of 6 p.m. To me, this is one of my most important meetings of the day and have rarely missed sitting down to dinner with my family in years. If I am going to be more than five minutes late for dinner I call my wife ahead of time and let her know I will be late.

Kids' activities – Every soccer game, badminton tournament, and school play go on my calendar. Only the most extreme situations interrupt my attending one of my kid's events.

Important spouse meetings – At times, my wife would have an important meeting which required me to be at home with the kids or to fill in with some of her duties. Whenever she has an important meeting requiring my assistance, she sends me an e-mail telling me of the meeting which I then put into my calendar.

No one ever said that your calendar was for work only. If it's important, put it on your calendar and treat it like an appointment. Don't allow your "busyness" at work to usurp the important non-work things you do.

Topic #2 - Is this me?

Review each question and ask yourself if the question sounds like something you have done or would do.

I have difficulty making it home in time for dinner with my loved ones

I get frustrated with colleagues who don't stay late at work like me

I have difficulty making time to attend loved one's events, i.e. school plays, sports activities

If left to my own devices, I would work most every waking moment of the day

Topic #3 – Measure success in results, not hours

In one of my leadership positions I worked with several senior managers who ran various parts of our organization. One senior manager could have been a poster child for workaholics anonymous. He would get to work by 7 a.m. and routinely stay until 7 p.m., then go home and be on e-mail until at least midnight. Weekends were little exception, with 8-10 hour days on the weekend a common occurrence. Aside from the fact that this senior manager was working himself into an early grave, he used the fact that he worked so many hours as both a badge of courage and a reason for raises and promotions. "I work longer and harder than anyone else in this place," he would frequently tell me. "I put in enough time for two people and should be compensated for it!" The trouble is, while he was working these horrendous hours, the results he delivered were not significantly different from his peer senior managers. He was measuring his success based on the number of hours he worked. I measured his success based on the results he delivered. He eventually left the group because I didn't "appreciate" him.

Let's compare two leaders. Leader A works just like my senior manager above and demonstrates his dedication through the number of hours he works. Leader B works much less than Leader A and delivers similar results as Leader B. All other things being equal, I have a greater respect for Leader B and would choose B over A as a leader in my organization. There are several very key factors which influence my thinking, as follows:

Leader A may be faster in a sprint, but Leader B will win a marathon – Leader A may work harder out of the gates and may put in more hours, but it will be only a matter of time before A runs out of gas and becomes less effective than B. This can manifest itself in reduced productivity, an increase in mistakes, or a poor attitude.

Leader B is more effective at getting more done per hour than Leader A – Simply put, if someone gets the same amount of results out of a 50 hour week as someone else who works 80 hours per week, I'd rather have the more effective leader on my team.

Leader B will scale better than Leader A – Every time I've worked with a highly effective leader B, he has been able to take on greater responsibility and bigger problems more effectively than an A. The A leader will tend to think in terms of, "How can I get this done?" where the B leader will tend to think in terms of, "Who can help me do this?"

When you add all of this up, those who measure success based on hours worked will prioritize hours over results and will be less motivated to figure out how to get more work done in less time. Those who measure success based on results are more likely to figure out better ways to do things, prioritize their work, and get home in time for dinner.

So what is working "too much?" This varies dramatically based on your culture, industry, and tolerance for work. I've tended to get into a "happy place" working between 45-50 hours per week. Your mileage may vary. I know some people who are comfortable and have good work/life balance at 50-55 hours per week and then there are others who are completely exhausted if they work 40 hours per week. Your responsibility is to find your "happy place" where you are delivering results and making good time for non-work activities.

The point here is simple; don't use the clock as your gauge of success; use the results you deliver as your success yardstick.

Topic #3 – Is this me?

Review each question and ask yourself if the question sounds like something you have done or would do.

When I get an additional assignment I typically will just work more hours to try to get it done versus prioritizing work or looking for help

It bothers me when others don't work as many hours as I do

I have been upset when someone who doesn't work as many hours as me gets chosen for promotion over me

I believe to get ahead I have to work at least 60 hours per week

Topic #4 – Don't voluntarily succumb to peer pressure

I had the opportunity to work "on loan" in another department in my company. At onset of my on-loan assignment, I began evaluating whether or not I might want to work in the department permanently. The work was very interesting, the team was very competent, and my skill sets fit well in the team. Things looked very promising . . . at first.

As I worked with the team over a period of two months, I noticed something very peculiar. It was very typical for the team to work until at least 9 p.m. The department manager would frequently schedule 7 p.m. meetings and expected that everyone would work those hours. I typically would get into work around 6 a.m. and would leave around 5 p.m. Thus, I was missing a lot of the department manager's meetings and would need to get up to speed at a later date. I took a bit of heat from my teammates because I was working "banker's hours." Despite the fact that I really enjoyed the work and what the team was doing, I decided not to join the department because I was unwilling to take on the work pattern that the department demanded. In hindsight, it was a great decision because I was able to keep better check on my work/life balance by not moving to the new department.

From our earliest years, we are exposed to peer pressure. The "I dare you's" from our youth become "Who's got a bigger house" or "Who drives a nicer car" as adults. Unfortunately, the work environment is not exempt from peer pressure. Whether inflicted by ourselves or others, many of us feel pressure to out-perform colleagues and work longer and harder to be on top. Now, I've got nothing against good, healthy competition. When people constructively compete, it raises the level of play for the entire team and causes others to improve as well.

The question comes when you deciding where you want to compete and where you'll concede. I decided long ago that trying to keep up with the hours some of my peers worked was not the way to compete in the workplace. I have conceded the hours race in favor of having better work/life balance. At times, I've taken some heat for not physically being at work as many hours as some of my colleagues even though my results were there. I've decided that I'm not going to care about running the hours race and have joyfully thrown in the towel on the "Who works more hours" game. Interestingly enough, I've never felt for a moment that my career has been hurt since I've chosen not to keep up with the Joneses on the hours race.

Look, just because a peer works 18 hours a day doesn't mean he or she gets more done or is more effective. It just means that your peer chooses to run the hours race because he or she feels it is the best means to get ahead. Don't let your peers' actions pressure you to run the wrong race. Just stay focused on providing meaningful results that provide value to the organization.

Topic #4 - Is this me?

Review each question and ask yourself if the question sounds like something you have done or would do.

I feel guilty if I leave early and others are still at work

I feel I have to work as many hours as my manager works

I feel as if I am "missing out" if something happens at work and I am not there to respond

I at times compare how many hours I work with how many hours others work

Topic #5 – Don't take on too much "life" in work/life balance

Our son is mainstream autistic. He is very high functioning and has aspirations of being a movie director when he grows up. When he was diagnosed as a toddler, we had to learn about some of his quirks and how to make our home life workable for him. One thing we learned early on was his need for stability in the home and a simple, predictable

schedule. We adopted a very stable home schedule where we ate dinner at the same time every night, went to bed at the same time every night, and did not have a lot of spontaneous activities. Our spontaneity needed to be planned (sounds like an oxymoron, I know!) to where we would give our son warnings before doing something which broke routine.

As we adjusted into this scheduled lifestyle, we became aware of some interesting benefits. The first is that our home life appeared to be much less hectic than that of many of our friends. The second is that we never once felt as if we were "missing out" on life because of our scheduled lifestyle. We to this day do a lot of very fun activities, it just requires a bit of advance planning and giving our son some warning that there will be a change in schedule. Our big lesson learned through our migration to a scheduled lifestyle is not to cram too much "life" into work/life balance.

Look, achieving work/life balance doesn't mean you cram more and more stuff into the life side of the equation to balance out a high-octane work life. Achieving good work/life balance means doing both in moderation and minimizing the stress in your life. You could be working a 40-hour work week and still be stressed out because of the non-work activities you've committed to. So, rather than get your stress from the work side of the equation, you get it from life side. Regardless of where it comes from, stress is stress and will ultimately spread to other areas of your life.

The point here is clear: work/life balance is best achieved when your stress level is minimized. Doing too much life can be just as stressful to you and your loved ones as doing too much work. Don't feel obligated or pressured to fill up every hour of your week with life activities. Doing both in moderation helps you attain the key benefit of work/life balance; a low-stress life.

Topic #5 - Is this me?

Review each question and ask yourself if the question sounds like something you have done or would do.

I just don't feel rested

My non-work hours feel just as busy as my work hours

I believe in a work-hard, play-hard lifestyle

I tend to over-commit myself when it comes to non-work activities

Putting it into action

So you've gone through each topic and assessed yourself against some key questions. What next?

The next step is to develop a Personal Action Plan based on the results of your self-assessment. First, decide which 1-3 focus topics to address. Then decide on up to three tangible actions for each focus item to help you create new habits. As input to the tangible actions, use the ideas matrix in this section to help jump-start some creative ways to address your focus topics.

Here are some things to consider as you're developing your Personal Action Plan:

Make sure your actions are clear, concise, tangible, and easy to understand.

Keep your focus topics to no more than three areas. Trying to work with too many focus topics will dilute your efforts and reduce your likelihood of success.

Keep your actions to no more than three per focus topic. As with focus topics, the more actions you try to take on, the less likely you'll do any of them well (if at all). Get very precise on a few actions and nail them.

Be realistic. Don't get overly aggressive with your action items and set yourself up for failure. Pick a few precise, high-impact reasonable actions and execute.

Your action plan should be personal, relevant, and applicable to you and your position. No one can or should develop an action plan for you. The best action plans are developed by the owner and utilize at least one coach (a trusted colleague, team member, or family member) who can observe you "in action" and help you build new habits.

As food for thought, use the following list of ideas to help you jump-start your action plan. You may use some or none of the below ideas, just make sure your actions are personal, relevant and applicable to you.

Consciously (and honestly) decide what is really important

For the next two weeks, keep a detailed log of where you spend your time. Categorize your time into "work" and "non-work" categories. At the end of two weeks, add up the time and assess if you are spending time in line with your priorities.

Interview several people that have exposure to both your work and non-work habits. Ask them for honest and direct feedback on where they see you focusing your attention.

Spend some time in discussion with your spouse or significant other on what your mutual objectives are regarding work/life balance. Document the objectives and review the objectives together monthly to assess how well you both are adhering to the objectives

Make your calendar a life thing, not just a work thing

At the beginning of each week, review your calendar and schedule important non-work activities, i.e. exercise or dinner time

Schedule some regular "open time" in your calendar; time that you block out in your calendar that you can spend on non-work activities

Schedule all loved one activities into your calendar as soon as the dates of the activities are known, i.e. if your child plays soccer, put all of the soccer games in your calendar as soon as you receive the schedule

Ask your spouse or significant other to hold you accountable for meeting non-work commitments in your calendar. Try doing a weekly review with your spouse or significant other and getting feedback on how well you are doing with non-work commitments.

Measure success in results, not hours

For each assignment you receive, get a concrete picture on what successful completion means and what the deliverable needs to look like. If necessary, discuss with your manager to ensure agreement on the deliverable

Evaluate each aspect of your existing job and ask yourself the following questions:

- How can I get this aspect of my job done more efficiently?

- Who can help me get my job done better?

- Am I working too hard to "polish the apple" (continuing to work on something longer than necessary)?

For a period of a month, force yourself to work no more than 45 hours per week. At the end of the month, evaluate your results against prior months

Don't voluntarily succumb to peer pressure

Adopt a "just say no" mantra when you catch yourself comparing hours worked with colleagues.

Set and agree upon the expectation with your manager on hours you will be keeping

Commit to being home at a specific time each night and allow for a spouse or significant other to hold you accountable for the commitment

Don't take on too much "life" in work/life balance

Make a list of all of your non-work commitments and the approximate number of hours per week the commitment requires. Decide if there are commitments which should be terminated.

Block out "relax times" on your schedule where you will do just that; relax and do something calming and stress-free

Consciously schedule all of your non-work commitments and activities into your calendar, including those commitments that are recurring

Discuss with your spouse or significant other a reasonable amount of non-work activities which you will take on and decide together what things you will say "yes" to and which you will say "no"

Some final thoughts

Change is hard. Change takes time. Change can be frustrating. But change for the better is always worth it.

Be patient with yourself.

Don't take on too much at once; focus on just one or two things and do them well.

Use a trusted friend or advisor to help you in your change journey.

You have to really want to change for it to happen. If you don't want it don't bother doing it.

Don't give up. You won't regret it.

About the Author

Lonnie Pacelli is an internationally recognized project management and leadership development expert with over 30 years' experience working with Fortune 100 organizations. His no-nonsense style helps get to the root of problems quickly and delivers sustainable results.

Find out more about Lonnie at LonniePacelli.com